C-2245     CAREER EXAMINATION SERIES

*This is your*
*PASSBOOK for...*

# Paralegal Aide

*Test Preparation Study Guide*
*Questions & Answers*

# COPYRIGHT NOTICE

This book is SOLELY intended for, is sold ONLY to, and its use is RESTRICTED to individual, bona fide applicants or candidates who qualify by virtue of having seriously filed applications for appropriate license, certificate, professional and/or promotional advancement, higher school matriculation, scholarship, or other legitimate requirements of education and/or governmental authorities.

This book is NOT intended for use, class instruction, tutoring, training, duplication, copying, reprinting, excerption, or adaptation, etc., by:

1) Other publishers
2) Proprietors and/or Instructors of "Coaching" and/or Preparatory Courses
3) Personnel and/or Training Divisions of commercial, industrial, and governmental organizations
4) Schools, colleges, or universities and/or their departments and staffs, including teachers and other personnel
5) Testing Agencies or Bureaus
6) Study groups which seek by the purchase of a single volume to copy and/or duplicate and/or adapt this material for use by the group as a whole without having purchased individual volumes for each of the members of the group
7) Et al.

Such persons would be in violation of appropriate Federal and State statutes.

PROVISION OF LICENSING AGREEMENTS – Recognized educational, commercial, industrial, and governmental institutions and organizations, and others legitimately engaged in educational pursuits, including training, testing, and measurement activities, may address request for a licensing agreement to the copyright owners, who will determine whether, and under what conditions, including fees and charges, the materials in this book may be used them.  In other words, a licensing facility exists for the legitimate use of the material in this book on other than an individual basis.  However, it is asseverated and affirmed here that the material in this book CANNOT be used without the receipt of the express permission of such a licensing agreement from the Publishers. Inquiries re licensing should be addressed to the company, attention rights and permissions department.

All rights reserved, including the right of reproduction in whole or in part, in any form or by any means, electronic or mechanical, including photocopying, recording, or by any information storage and retrieval system, without permission in writing from the Publisher.

Copyright © 2024 by
## National Learning Corporation

212 Michael Drive, Syosset, NY 11791
(516) 921-8888 • www.passbooks.com
E-mail: info@passbooks.com

PUBLISHED IN THE UNITED STATES OF AMERICA

# PASSBOOK® SERIES

THE *PASSBOOK® SERIES* has been created to prepare applicants and candidates for the ultimate academic battlefield – the examination room.

At some time in our lives, each and every one of us may be required to take an examination – for validation, matriculation, admission, qualification, registration, certification, or licensure.

Based on the assumption that every applicant or candidate has met the basic formal educational standards, has taken the required number of courses, and read the necessary texts, the *PASSBOOK® SERIES* furnishes the one special preparation which may assure passing with confidence, instead of failing with insecurity. Examination questions – together with answers – are furnished as the basic vehicle for study so that the mysteries of the examination and its compounding difficulties may be eliminated or diminished by a sure method.

This book is meant to help you pass your examination provided that you qualify and are serious in your objective.

The entire field is reviewed through the huge store of content information which is succinctly presented through a provocative and challenging approach – the question-and-answer method.

A climate of success is established by furnishing the correct answers at the end of each test.

You soon learn to recognize types of questions, forms of questions, and patterns of questioning. You may even begin to anticipate expected outcomes.

You perceive that many questions are repeated or adapted so that you can gain acute insights, which may enable you to score many sure points.

You learn how to confront new questions, or types of questions, and to attack them confidently and work out the correct answers.

You note objectives and emphases, and recognize pitfalls and dangers, so that you may make positive educational adjustments.

Moreover, you are kept fully informed in relation to new concepts, methods, practices, and directions in the field.

You discover that you are actually taking the examination all the time: you are preparing for the examination by "taking" an examination, not by reading extraneous and/or supererogatory textbooks.

In short, this PASSBOOK®, used directedly, should be an important factor in helping you to pass your test.

# PARALEGAL AIDE

## DUTIES AND RESPONSIBILITIES

The work involves responsibility for performing paralegal duties and a variety of tasks that while not requiring the skills of an attorney, nevertheless, entail the application of limited legal procedures and research techniques to facilitate the preparation of legal documents and matters for litigation. Depending upon the department involved, the incumbent's specific duties will vary within the broad framework of paralegal skills. The work is reformed under the general supervision of the department's attorneys with considerable leeway allowed for the exercise of independent judgement. Paralegal Aides assist and receive training from attorneys, formal referees and more experienced Paralegal Aides in the management of cases through various stages of legal proceedings; may draft legal papers for review by higher level staff and/or attorneys; independently perform routine paralegal tasks and may conduct legal research. All Paralegal Aides perform related work.

## EXAMPLES OF TYPICAL TASKS

Interviews clients, witnesses, victims and complainants; assists in the preparation and service of legal papers, e.g., motions, subpoenas, and other documents; performs legal research; collects, assembles and assists in evaluating evidence and technical data for use in trials and proceedings; prepares witnesses and arranges for appearance of witnesses at trials; maintains court calendars and schedules; may conduct investigations, examine and adjust claims and conduct closings on real estate titles and mortgages; may be responsible for the overall management of caseload; monitors case flow and movement; maintains control of all relevant information for the prosecution of a case; may collect and analyze data to determine the effectiveness of programs; monitors compliance with Federal and State guidelines for grant projects; prepares analyses of testimony; summarizes briefs and court decisions; prepares reports on individual cases or groups of cases; assists in all forms of legal proceedings, programs and projects.

## TESTS

The written test will be of the multiple-choice type and may include questions on preparing petitions, complaints, memoranda, motions and other complex legal documents; interviewing, dealing tactfully with and drawing usable information from various persons; following complex procedures in performing paralegal task, such as obtaining documents and evidence for trial; legal terminology; evaluating conclusions in light of known facts; understanding legal materials and laws and applying them to concrete situations; presenting ideas effectively in standard English; and other related areas.

# HOW TO TAKE A TEST

I. YOU MUST PASS AN EXAMINATION

A. *WHAT EVERY CANDIDATE SHOULD KNOW*

Examination applicants often ask us for help in preparing for the written test. What can I study in advance? What kinds of questions will be asked? How will the test be given? How will the papers be graded?

As an applicant for a civil service examination, you may be wondering about some of these things. Our purpose here is to suggest effective methods of advance study and to describe civil service examinations.

Your chances for success on this examination can be increased if you know how to prepare. Those "pre-examination jitters" can be reduced if you know what to expect. You can even experience an adventure in good citizenship if you know why civil service exams are given.

B. *WHY ARE CIVIL SERVICE EXAMINATIONS GIVEN?*

Civil service examinations are important to you in two ways. As a citizen, you want public jobs filled by employees who know how to do their work. As a job seeker, you want a fair chance to compete for that job on an equal footing with other candidates. The best-known means of accomplishing this two-fold goal is the competitive examination.

Exams are widely publicized throughout the nation. They may be administered for jobs in federal, state, city, municipal, town or village governments or agencies.

Any citizen may apply, with some limitations, such as the age or residence of applicants. Your experience and education may be reviewed to see whether you meet the requirements for the particular examination. When these requirements exist, they are reasonable and applied consistently to all applicants. Thus, a competitive examination may cause you some uneasiness now, but it is your privilege and safeguard.

C. *HOW ARE CIVIL SERVICE EXAMS DEVELOPED?*

Examinations are carefully written by trained technicians who are specialists in the field known as "psychological measurement," in consultation with recognized authorities in the field of work that the test will cover. These experts recommend the subject matter areas or skills to be tested; only those knowledges or skills important to your success on the job are included. The most reliable books and source materials available are used as references. Together, the experts and technicians judge the difficulty level of the questions.

Test technicians know how to phrase questions so that the problem is clearly stated. Their ethics do not permit "trick" or "catch" questions. Questions may have been tried out on sample groups, or subjected to statistical analysis, to determine their usefulness.

Written tests are often used in combination with performance tests, ratings of training and experience, and oral interviews. All of these measures combine to form the best-known means of finding the right person for the right job.

## II. HOW TO PASS THE WRITTEN TEST

### A. NATURE OF THE EXAMINATION

To prepare intelligently for civil service examinations, you should know how they differ from school examinations you have taken. In school you were assigned certain definite pages to read or subjects to cover. The examination questions were quite detailed and usually emphasized memory. Civil service exams, on the other hand, try to discover your present ability to perform the duties of a position, plus your potentiality to learn these duties. In other words, a civil service exam attempts to predict how successful you will be. Questions cover such a broad area that they cannot be as minute and detailed as school exam questions.

In the public service similar kinds of work, or positions, are grouped together in one "class." This process is known as *position-classification*. All the positions in a class are paid according to the salary range for that class. One class title covers all of these positions, and they are all tested by the same examination.

### B. FOUR BASIC STEPS

#### 1) Study the announcement

How, then, can you know what subjects to study? Our best answer is: "Learn as much as possible about the class of positions for which you've applied." The exam will test the knowledge, skills and abilities needed to do the work.

Your most valuable source of information about the position you want is the official exam announcement. This announcement lists the training and experience qualifications. Check these standards and apply only if you come reasonably close to meeting them.

The brief description of the position in the examination announcement offers some clues to the subjects which will be tested. Think about the job itself. Review the duties in your mind. Can you perform them, or are there some in which you are rusty? Fill in the blank spots in your preparation.

Many jurisdictions preview the written test in the exam announcement by including a section called "Knowledge and Abilities Required," "Scope of the Examination," or some similar heading. Here you will find out specifically what fields will be tested.

#### 2) Review your own background

Once you learn in general what the position is all about, and what you need to know to do the work, ask yourself which subjects you already know fairly well and which need improvement. You may wonder whether to concentrate on improving your strong areas or on building some background in your fields of weakness. When the announcement has specified "some knowledge" or "considerable knowledge," or has used adjectives like "beginning principles of..." or "advanced ... methods," you can get a clue as to the number and difficulty of questions to be asked in any given field. More questions, and hence broader coverage, would be included for those subjects which are more important in the work. Now weigh your strengths and weaknesses against the job requirements and prepare accordingly.

#### 3) Determine the level of the position

Another way to tell how intensively you should prepare is to understand the level of the job for which you are applying. Is it the entering level? In other words, is this the position in which beginners in a field of work are hired? Or is it an intermediate or advanced level? Sometimes this is indicated by such words as "Junior" or "Senior" in the class title. Other jurisdictions use Roman numerals to designate the level – Clerk I, Clerk II, for example. The word "Supervisor" sometimes appears in the title. If the level is not indicated by the title, check the description of duties. Will you be working under very close supervision, or will you have responsibility for independent decisions in this work?

**4) Choose appropriate study materials**

Now that you know the subjects to be examined and the relative amount of each subject to be covered, you can choose suitable study materials. For beginning level jobs, or even advanced ones, if you have a pronounced weakness in some aspect of your training, read a modern, standard textbook in that field. Be sure it is up to date and has general coverage. Such books are normally available at your library, and the librarian will be glad to help you locate one. For entry-level positions, questions of appropriate difficulty are chosen – neither highly advanced questions, nor those too simple. Such questions require careful thought but not advanced training.

If the position for which you are applying is technical or advanced, you will read more advanced, specialized material. If you are already familiar with the basic principles of your field, elementary textbooks would waste your time. Concentrate on advanced textbooks and technical periodicals. Think through the concepts and review difficult problems in your field.

These are all general sources. You can get more ideas on your own initiative, following these leads. For example, training manuals and publications of the government agency which employs workers in your field can be useful, particularly for technical and professional positions. A letter or visit to the government department involved may result in more specific study suggestions, and certainly will provide you with a more definite idea of the exact nature of the position you are seeking.


III. KINDS OF TESTS

Tests are used for purposes other than measuring knowledge and ability to perform specified duties. For some positions, it is equally important to test ability to make adjustments to new situations or to profit from training. In others, basic mental abilities not dependent on information are essential. Questions which test these things may not appear as pertinent to the duties of the position as those which test for knowledge and information. Yet they are often highly important parts of a fair examination. For very general questions, it is almost impossible to help you direct your study efforts. What we can do is to point out some of the more common of these general abilities needed in public service positions and describe some typical questions.

1) General information

Broad, general information has been found useful for predicting job success in some kinds of work. This is tested in a variety of ways, from vocabulary lists to questions about current events. Basic background in some field of work, such as sociology or economics, may be sampled in a group of questions. Often these are principles which have become familiar to most persons through exposure rather than through formal training. It is difficult to advise you how to study for these questions; being alert to the world around you is our best suggestion.

2) Verbal ability

An example of an ability needed in many positions is verbal or language ability. Verbal ability is, in brief, the ability to use and understand words. Vocabulary and grammar tests are typical measures of this ability. Reading comprehension or paragraph interpretation questions are common in many kinds of civil service tests. You are given a paragraph of written material and asked to find its central meaning.

3) Numerical ability

Number skills can be tested by the familiar arithmetic problem, by checking paired lists of numbers to see which are alike and which are different, or by interpreting charts and graphs. In the latter test, a graph may be printed in the test booklet which you are asked to use as the basis for answering questions.

4) Observation

A popular test for law-enforcement positions is the observation test. A picture is shown to you for several minutes, then taken away. Questions about the picture test your ability to observe both details and larger elements.

5) Following directions

In many positions in the public service, the employee must be able to carry out written instructions dependably and accurately. You may be given a chart with several columns, each column listing a variety of information. The questions require you to carry out directions involving the information given in the chart.

6) Skills and aptitudes

Performance tests effectively measure some manual skills and aptitudes. When the skill is one in which you are trained, such as typing or shorthand, you can practice. These tests are often very much like those given in business school or high school courses. For many of the other skills and aptitudes, however, no short-time preparation can be made. Skills and abilities natural to you or that you have developed throughout your lifetime are being tested.

Many of the general questions just described provide all the data needed to answer the questions and ask you to use your reasoning ability to find the answers. Your best preparation for these tests, as well as for tests of facts and ideas, is to be at your physical and mental best. You, no doubt, have your own methods of getting into an exam-taking mood and keeping "in shape." The next section lists some ideas on this subject.

IV. KINDS OF QUESTIONS

Only rarely is the "essay" question, which you answer in narrative form, used in civil service tests. Civil service tests are usually of the short-answer type. Full instructions for answering these questions will be given to you at the examination. But in case this is your first experience with short-answer questions and separate answer sheets, here is what you need to know:

**1) Multiple-choice Questions**

Most popular of the short-answer questions is the "multiple choice" or "best answer" question. It can be used, for example, to test for factual knowledge, ability to solve problems or judgment in meeting situations found at work.

A multiple-choice question is normally one of three types—
- It can begin with an incomplete statement followed by several possible endings. You are to find the one ending which *best* completes the statement, although some of the others may not be entirely wrong.
- It can also be a complete statement in the form of a question which is answered by choosing one of the statements listed.

- It can be in the form of a problem – again you select the best answer.

Here is an example of a multiple-choice question with a discussion which should give you some clues as to the method for choosing the right answer:

When an employee has a complaint about his assignment, the action which will *best* help him overcome his difficulty is to
- A. discuss his difficulty with his coworkers
- B. take the problem to the head of the organization
- C. take the problem to the person who gave him the assignment
- D. say nothing to anyone about his complaint

In answering this question, you should study each of the choices to find which is best. Consider choice "A" – Certainly an employee may discuss his complaint with fellow employees, but no change or improvement can result, and the complaint remains unresolved. Choice "B" is a poor choice since the head of the organization probably does not know what assignment you have been given, and taking your problem to him is known as "going over the head" of the supervisor. The supervisor, or person who made the assignment, is the person who can clarify it or correct any injustice. Choice "C" is, therefore, correct. To say nothing, as in choice "D," is unwise. Supervisors have and interest in knowing the problems employees are facing, and the employee is seeking a solution to his problem.

## 2) True/False Questions

The "true/false" or "right/wrong" form of question is sometimes used. Here a complete statement is given. Your job is to decide whether the statement is right or wrong.

SAMPLE: A roaming cell-phone call to a nearby city costs less than a non-roaming call to a distant city.

This statement is wrong, or false, since roaming calls are more expensive.

This is not a complete list of all possible question forms, although most of the others are variations of these common types. You will always get complete directions for answering questions. Be sure you understand *how* to mark your answers – ask questions until you do.

## V. RECORDING YOUR ANSWERS

Computer terminals are used more and more today for many different kinds of exams.
For an examination with very few applicants, you may be told to record your answers in the test booklet itself. Separate answer sheets are much more common. If this separate answer sheet is to be scored by machine – and this is often the case – it is highly important that you mark your answers correctly in order to get credit.
An electronic scoring machine is often used in civil service offices because of the speed with which papers can be scored. Machine-scored answer sheets must be marked with a pencil, which will be given to you. This pencil has a high graphite content which responds to the electronic scoring machine. As a matter of fact, stray dots may register as answers, so do not let your pencil rest on the answer sheet while you are pondering the correct answer. Also, if your pencil lead breaks or is otherwise defective, ask for another.

Since the answer sheet will be dropped in a slot in the scoring machine, be careful not to bend the corners or get the paper crumpled.

The answer sheet normally has five vertical columns of numbers, with 30 numbers to a column. These numbers correspond to the question numbers in your test booklet. After each number, going across the page are four or five pairs of dotted lines. These short dotted lines have small letters or numbers above them. The first two pairs may also have a "T" or "F" above the letters. This indicates that the first two pairs only are to be used if the questions are of the true-false type. If the questions are multiple choice, disregard the "T" and "F" and pay attention only to the small letters or numbers.

Answer your questions in the manner of the sample that follows:

32. The largest city in the United States is
    A. Washington, D.C.
    B. New York City
    C. Chicago
    D. Detroit
    E. San Francisco

1) Choose the answer you think is best. (New York City is the largest, so "B" is correct.)
2) Find the row of dotted lines numbered the same as the question you are answering. (Find row number 32)
3) Find the pair of dotted lines corresponding to the answer. (Find the pair of lines under the mark "B.")
4) Make a solid black mark between the dotted lines.

## VI. BEFORE THE TEST

Common sense will help you find procedures to follow to get ready for an examination. Too many of us, however, overlook these sensible measures. Indeed, nervousness and fatigue have been found to be the most serious reasons why applicants fail to do their best on civil service tests. Here is a list of reminders:

- Begin your preparation early – Don't wait until the last minute to go scurrying around for books and materials or to find out what the position is all about.
- Prepare continuously – An hour a night for a week is better than an all-night cram session. This has been definitely established. What is more, a night a week for a month will return better dividends than crowding your study into a shorter period of time.
- Locate the place of the exam – You have been sent a notice telling you when and where to report for the examination. If the location is in a different town or otherwise unfamiliar to you, it would be well to inquire the best route and learn something about the building.
- Relax the night before the test – Allow your mind to rest. Do not study at all that night. Plan some mild recreation or diversion; then go to bed early and get a good night's sleep.
- Get up early enough to make a leisurely trip to the place for the test – This way unforeseen events, traffic snarls, unfamiliar buildings, etc. will not upset you.
- Dress comfortably – A written test is not a fashion show. You will be known by number and not by name, so wear something comfortable.

- Leave excess paraphernalia at home – Shopping bags and odd bundles will get in your way. You need bring only the items mentioned in the official notice you received; usually everything you need is provided. Do not bring reference books to the exam. They will only confuse those last minutes and be taken away from you when in the test room.
- Arrive somewhat ahead of time – If because of transportation schedules you must get there very early, bring a newspaper or magazine to take your mind off yourself while waiting.
- Locate the examination room – When you have found the proper room, you will be directed to the seat or part of the room where you will sit. Sometimes you are given a sheet of instructions to read while you are waiting. Do not fill out any forms until you are told to do so; just read them and be prepared.
- Relax and prepare to listen to the instructions
- If you have any physical problem that may keep you from doing your best, be sure to tell the test administrator. If you are sick or in poor health, you really cannot do your best on the exam. You can come back and take the test some other time.

## VII. AT THE TEST

The day of the test is here and you have the test booklet in your hand. The temptation to get going is very strong. Caution! There is more to success than knowing the right answers. You must know how to identify your papers and understand variations in the type of short-answer question used in this particular examination. Follow these suggestions for maximum results from your efforts:

### 1) Cooperate with the monitor

The test administrator has a duty to create a situation in which you can be as much at ease as possible. He will give instructions, tell you when to begin, check to see that you are marking your answer sheet correctly, and so on. He is not there to guard you, although he will see that your competitors do not take unfair advantage. He wants to help you do your best.

### 2) Listen to all instructions

Don't jump the gun! Wait until you understand all directions. In most civil service tests you get more time than you need to answer the questions. So don't be in a hurry. Read each word of instructions until you clearly understand the meaning. Study the examples, listen to all announcements and follow directions. Ask questions if you do not understand what to do.

### 3) Identify your papers

Civil service exams are usually identified by number only. You will be assigned a number; you must not put your name on your test papers. Be sure to copy your number correctly. Since more than one exam may be given, copy your exact examination title.

### 4) Plan your time

Unless you are told that a test is a "speed" or "rate of work" test, speed itself is usually not important. Time enough to answer all the questions will be provided, but this does not mean that you have all day. An overall time limit has been set. Divide the total time (in minutes) by the number of questions to determine the approximate time you have for each question.

### 5) Do not linger over difficult questions

If you come across a difficult question, mark it with a paper clip (useful to have along) and come back to it when you have been through the booklet. One caution if you do this – be sure to skip a number on your answer sheet as well. Check often to be sure that you have not lost your place and that you are marking in the row numbered the same as the question you are answering.

### 6) Read the questions

Be sure you know what the question asks! Many capable people are unsuccessful because they failed to *read* the questions correctly.

### 7) Answer all questions

Unless you have been instructed that a penalty will be deducted for incorrect answers, it is better to guess than to omit a question.

### 8) Speed tests

It is often better NOT to guess on speed tests. It has been found that on timed tests people are tempted to spend the last few seconds before time is called in marking answers at random – without even reading them – in the hope of picking up a few extra points. To discourage this practice, the instructions may warn you that your score will be "corrected" for guessing. That is, a penalty will be applied. The incorrect answers will be deducted from the correct ones, or some other penalty formula will be used.

### 9) Review your answers

If you finish before time is called, go back to the questions you guessed or omitted to give them further thought. Review other answers if you have time.

### 10) Return your test materials

If you are ready to leave before others have finished or time is called, take ALL your materials to the monitor and leave quietly. Never take any test material with you. The monitor can discover whose papers are not complete, and taking a test booklet may be grounds for disqualification.

## VIII. EXAMINATION TECHNIQUES

1) Read the general instructions carefully. These are usually printed on the first page of the exam booklet. As a rule, these instructions refer to the timing of the examination; the fact that you should not start work until the signal and must stop work at a signal, etc. If there are any *special* instructions, such as a choice of questions to be answered, make sure that you note this instruction carefully.

2) When you are ready to start work on the examination, that is as soon as the signal has been given, read the instructions to each question booklet, underline any key words or phrases, such as *least, best, outline, describe* and the like. In this way you will tend to answer as requested rather than discover on reviewing your paper that you *listed without describing*, that you selected the *worst* choice rather than the *best* choice, etc.

3) If the examination is of the objective or multiple-choice type – that is, each question will also give a series of possible answers: A, B, C or D, and you are called upon to select the best answer and write the letter next to that answer on your answer paper – it is advisable to start answering each question in turn. There may be anywhere from 50 to 100 such questions in the three or four hours allotted and you can see how much time would be taken if you read through all the questions before beginning to answer any. Furthermore, if you come across a question or group of questions which you know would be difficult to answer, it would undoubtedly affect your handling of all the other questions.

4) If the examination is of the essay type and contains but a few questions, it is a moot point as to whether you should read all the questions before starting to answer any one. Of course, if you are given a choice – say five out of seven and the like – then it is essential to read all the questions so you can eliminate the two that are most difficult. If, however, you are asked to answer all the questions, there may be danger in trying to answer the easiest one first because you may find that you will spend too much time on it. The best technique is to answer the first question, then proceed to the second, etc.

5) Time your answers. Before the exam begins, write down the time it started, then add the time allowed for the examination and write down the time it must be completed, then divide the time available somewhat as follows:
   - If 3-1/2 hours are allowed, that would be 210 minutes. If you have 80 objective-type questions, that would be an average of 2-1/2 minutes per question. Allow yourself no more than 2 minutes per question, or a total of 160 minutes, which will permit about 50 minutes to review.
   - If for the time allotment of 210 minutes there are 7 essay questions to answer, that would average about 30 minutes a question. Give yourself only 25 minutes per question so that you have about 35 minutes to review.

6) The most important instruction is to *read each question* and make sure you know what is wanted. The second most important instruction is to *time yourself properly* so that you answer every question. The third most important instruction is to *answer every question*. Guess if you have to but include something for each question. Remember that you will receive no credit for a blank and will probably receive some credit if you write something in answer to an essay question. If you guess a letter – say "B" for a multiple-choice question – you may have guessed right. If you leave a blank as an answer to a multiple-choice question, the examiners may respect your feelings but it will not add a point to your score. Some exams may penalize you for wrong answers, so in such cases *only*, you may not want to guess unless you have some basis for your answer.

7) Suggestions
   a. Objective-type questions
      1. Examine the question booklet for proper sequence of pages and questions
      2. Read all instructions carefully
      3. Skip any question which seems too difficult; return to it after all other questions have been answered
      4. Apportion your time properly; do not spend too much time on any single question or group of questions

5. Note and underline key words – *all, most, fewest, least, best, worst, same, opposite,* etc.
6. Pay particular attention to negatives
7. Note unusual option, e.g., unduly long, short, complex, different or similar in content to the body of the question
8. Observe the use of "hedging" words – *probably, may, most likely,* etc.
9. Make sure that your answer is put next to the same number as the question
10. Do not second-guess unless you have good reason to believe the second answer is definitely more correct
11. Cross out original answer if you decide another answer is more accurate; do not erase until you are ready to hand your paper in
12. Answer all questions; guess unless instructed otherwise
13. Leave time for review

   b. Essay questions
      1. Read each question carefully
      2. Determine exactly what is wanted. Underline key words or phrases.
      3. Decide on outline or paragraph answer
      4. Include many different points and elements unless asked to develop any one or two points or elements
      5. Show impartiality by giving pros and cons unless directed to select one side only
      6. Make and write down any assumptions you find necessary to answer the questions
      7. Watch your English, grammar, punctuation and choice of words
      8. Time your answers; don't crowd material

8) Answering the essay question

Most essay questions can be answered by framing the specific response around several key words or ideas. Here are a few such key words or ideas:

M's: manpower, materials, methods, money, management
P's: purpose, program, policy, plan, procedure, practice, problems, pitfalls, personnel, public relations

   a. Six basic steps in handling problems:
      1. Preliminary plan and background development
      2. Collect information, data and facts
      3. Analyze and interpret information, data and facts
      4. Analyze and develop solutions as well as make recommendations
      5. Prepare report and sell recommendations
      6. Install recommendations and follow up effectiveness

   b. Pitfalls to avoid
      1. *Taking things for granted* – A statement of the situation does not necessarily imply that each of the elements is necessarily true; for example, a complaint may be invalid and biased so that all that can be taken for granted is that a complaint has been registered

2. *Considering only one side of a situation* – Wherever possible, indicate several alternatives and then point out the reasons you selected the best one
3. *Failing to indicate follow up* – Whenever your answer indicates action on your part, make certain that you will take proper follow-up action to see how successful your recommendations, procedures or actions turn out to be
4. *Taking too long in answering any single question* – Remember to time your answers properly

## IX. AFTER THE TEST

Scoring procedures differ in detail among civil service jurisdictions although the general principles are the same. Whether the papers are hand-scored or graded by machine we have described, they are nearly always graded by number. That is, the person who marks the paper knows only the number – never the name – of the applicant. Not until all the papers have been graded will they be matched with names. If other tests, such as training and experience or oral interview ratings have been given, scores will be combined. Different parts of the examination usually have different weights. For example, the written test might count 60 percent of the final grade, and a rating of training and experience 40 percent. In many jurisdictions, veterans will have a certain number of points added to their grades.

After the final grade has been determined, the names are placed in grade order and an eligible list is established. There are various methods for resolving ties between those who get the same final grade – probably the most common is to place first the name of the person whose application was received first. Job offers are made from the eligible list in the order the names appear on it. You will be notified of your grade and your rank as soon as all these computations have been made. This will be done as rapidly as possible.

People who are found to meet the requirements in the announcement are called "eligibles." Their names are put on a list of eligible candidates. An eligible's chances of getting a job depend on how high he stands on this list and how fast agencies are filling jobs from the list.

When a job is to be filled from a list of eligibles, the agency asks for the names of people on the list of eligibles for that job. When the civil service commission receives this request, it sends to the agency the names of the three people highest on this list. Or, if the job to be filled has specialized requirements, the office sends the agency the names of the top three persons who meet these requirements from the general list.

The appointing officer makes a choice from among the three people whose names were sent to him. If the selected person accepts the appointment, the names of the others are put back on the list to be considered for future openings.

That is the rule in hiring from all kinds of eligible lists, whether they are for typist, carpenter, chemist, or something else. For every vacancy, the appointing officer has his choice of any one of the top three eligibles on the list. This explains why the person whose name is on top of the list sometimes does not get an appointment when some of the persons lower on the list do. If the appointing officer chooses the second or third eligible, the No. 1 eligible does not get a job at once, but stays on the list until he is appointed or the list is terminated.

# X. HOW TO PASS THE INTERVIEW TEST

The examination for which you applied requires an oral interview test. You have already taken the written test and you are now being called for the interview test – the final part of the formal examination.

You may think that it is not possible to prepare for an interview test and that there are no procedures to follow during an interview. Our purpose is to point out some things you can do in advance that will help you and some good rules to follow and pitfalls to avoid while you are being interviewed.

*What is an interview supposed to test?*

The written examination is designed to test the technical knowledge and competence of the candidate; the oral is designed to evaluate intangible qualities, not readily measured otherwise, and to establish a list showing the relative fitness of each candidate – as measured against his competitors – for the position sought. Scoring is not on the basis of "right" and "wrong," but on a sliding scale of values ranging from "not passable" to "outstanding." As a matter of fact, it is possible to achieve a relatively low score without a single "incorrect" answer because of evident weakness in the qualities being measured.

Occasionally, an examination may consist entirely of an oral test – either an individual or a group oral. In such cases, information is sought concerning the technical knowledges and abilities of the candidate, since there has been no written examination for this purpose. More commonly, however, an oral test is used to supplement a written examination.

*Who conducts interviews?*

The composition of oral boards varies among different jurisdictions. In nearly all, a representative of the personnel department serves as chairman. One of the members of the board may be a representative of the department in which the candidate would work. In some cases, "outside experts" are used, and, frequently, a businessman or some other representative of the general public is asked to serve. Labor and management or other special groups may be represented. The aim is to secure the services of experts in the appropriate field.

However the board is composed, it is a good idea (and not at all improper or unethical) to ascertain in advance of the interview who the members are and what groups they represent. When you are introduced to them, you will have some idea of their backgrounds and interests, and at least you will not stutter and stammer over their names.

*What should be done before the interview?*

While knowledge about the board members is useful and takes some of the surprise element out of the interview, there is other preparation which is more substantive. It *is* possible to prepare for an oral interview – in several ways:

**1) Keep a copy of your application and review it carefully before the interview**

This may be the only document before the oral board, and the starting point of the interview. Know what education and experience you have listed there, and the sequence and dates of all of it. Sometimes the board will ask you to review the highlights of your experience for them; you should not have to hem and haw doing it.

**2) Study the class specification and the examination announcement**

Usually, the oral board has one or both of these to guide them. The qualities, characteristics or knowledges required by the position sought are stated in these documents. They offer valuable clues as to the nature of the oral interview. For example, if the job involves supervisory responsibilities, the announcement will usually indicate that knowledge of modern supervisory methods and the qualifications of the candidate as a supervisor will be tested. If so, you can expect such questions, frequently in the form of a hypothetical situation which you are expected to solve. NEVER go into an oral without knowledge of the duties and responsibilities of the job you seek.

### 3) Think through each qualification required

Try to visualize the kind of questions you would ask if you were a board member. How well could you answer them? Try especially to appraise your own knowledge and background in each area, *measured against the job sought*, and identify any areas in which you are weak. Be critical and realistic – do not flatter yourself.

### 4) Do some general reading in areas in which you feel you may be weak

For example, if the job involves supervision and your past experience has NOT, some general reading in supervisory methods and practices, particularly in the field of human relations, might be useful. Do NOT study agency procedures or detailed manuals. The oral board will be testing your understanding and capacity, not your memory.

### 5) Get a good night's sleep and watch your general health and mental attitude

You will want a clear head at the interview. Take care of a cold or any other minor ailment, and of course, no hangovers.

*What should be done on the day of the interview?*

Now comes the day of the interview itself. Give yourself plenty of time to get there. Plan to arrive somewhat ahead of the scheduled time, particularly if your appointment is in the fore part of the day. If a previous candidate fails to appear, the board might be ready for you a bit early. By early afternoon an oral board is almost invariably behind schedule if there are many candidates, and you may have to wait. Take along a book or magazine to read, or your application to review, but leave any extraneous material in the waiting room when you go in for your interview. In any event, relax and compose yourself.

The matter of dress is important. The board is forming impressions about you – from your experience, your manners, your attitude, and your appearance. Give your personal appearance careful attention. Dress your best, but not your flashiest. Choose conservative, appropriate clothing, and be sure it is immaculate. This is a business interview, and your appearance should indicate that you regard it as such. Besides, being well groomed and properly dressed will help boost your confidence.

Sooner or later, someone will call your name and escort you into the interview room. *This is it.* From here on you are on your own. It is too late for any more preparation. But remember, you asked for this opportunity to prove your fitness, and you are here because your request was granted.

*What happens when you go in?*

The usual sequence of events will be as follows: The clerk (who is often the board stenographer) will introduce you to the chairman of the oral board, who will introduce you to the other members of the board. Acknowledge the introductions before you sit down. Do not be surprised if you find a microphone facing you or a stenotypist sitting by. Oral interviews are usually recorded in the event of an appeal or other review.

Usually the chairman of the board will open the interview by reviewing the highlights of your education and work experience from your application – primarily for the benefit of the other members of the board, as well as to get the material into the record. Do not interrupt or comment unless there is an error or significant misinterpretation; if that is the case, do not hesitate. But do not quibble about insignificant matters. Also, he will usually ask you some question about your education, experience or your present job – partly to get you to start talking and to establish the interviewing "rapport." He may start the actual questioning, or turn it over to one of the other members. Frequently, each member undertakes the questioning on a particular area, one in which he is perhaps most competent, so you can expect each member to participate in the examination. Because time is limited, you may also expect some rather abrupt switches in the direction the questioning takes, so do not be upset by it. Normally, a board member will not pursue a single line of questioning unless he discovers a particular strength or weakness.

After each member has participated, the chairman will usually ask whether any member has any further questions, then will ask you if you have anything you wish to add. Unless you are expecting this question, it may floor you. Worse, it may start you off on an extended, extemporaneous speech. The board is not usually seeking more information. The question is principally to offer you a last opportunity to present further qualifications or to indicate that you have nothing to add. So, if you feel that a significant qualification or characteristic has been overlooked, it is proper to point it out in a sentence or so. Do not compliment the board on the thoroughness of their examination – they have been sketchy, and you know it. If you wish, merely say, "No thank you, I have nothing further to add." This is a point where you can "talk yourself out" of a good impression or fail to present an important bit of information. Remember, *you close the interview yourself.*

The chairman will then say, "That is all, Mr. _____, thank you." Do not be startled; the interview is over, and quicker than you think. Thank him, gather your belongings and take your leave. Save your sigh of relief for the other side of the door.


*How to put your best foot forward*
Throughout this entire process, you may feel that the board individually and collectively is trying to pierce your defenses, seek out your hidden weaknesses and embarrass and confuse you. Actually, this is not true. They are obliged to make an appraisal of your qualifications for the job you are seeking, and they want to see you in your best light. Remember, they must interview all candidates and a non-cooperative candidate may become a failure in spite of their best efforts to bring out his qualifications. Here are 15 suggestions that will help you:

**1) Be natural – Keep your attitude confident, not cocky**
If you are not confident that you can do the job, do not expect the board to be. Do not apologize for your weaknesses, try to bring out your strong points. The board is interested in a positive, not negative, presentation. Cockiness will antagonize any board member and make him wonder if you are covering up a weakness by a false show of strength.

**2) Get comfortable, but don't lounge or sprawl**
Sit erectly but not stiffly. A careless posture may lead the board to conclude that you are careless in other things, or at least that you are not impressed by the importance of the occasion. Either conclusion is natural, even if incorrect. Do not fuss with your clothing, a pencil or an ashtray. Your hands may occasionally be useful to emphasize a point; do not let them become a point of distraction.

**3) Do not wisecrack or make small talk**
This is a serious situation, and your attitude should show that you consider it as such. Further, the time of the board is limited – they do not want to waste it, and neither should you.

### 4) Do not exaggerate your experience or abilities

In the first place, from information in the application or other interviews and sources, the board may know more about you than you think. Secondly, you probably will not get away with it. An experienced board is rather adept at spotting such a situation, so do not take the chance.

### 5) If you know a board member, do not make a point of it, yet do not hide it

Certainly you are not fooling him, and probably not the other members of the board. Do not try to take advantage of your acquaintanceship – it will probably do you little good.

### 6) Do not dominate the interview

Let the board do that. They will give you the clues – do not assume that you have to do all the talking. Realize that the board has a number of questions to ask you, and do not try to take up all the interview time by showing off your extensive knowledge of the answer to the first one.

### 7) Be attentive

You only have 20 minutes or so, and you should keep your attention at its sharpest throughout. When a member is addressing a problem or question to you, give him your undivided attention. Address your reply principally to him, but do not exclude the other board members.

### 8) Do not interrupt

A board member may be stating a problem for you to analyze. He will ask you a question when the time comes. Let him state the problem, and wait for the question.

### 9) Make sure you understand the question

Do not try to answer until you are sure what the question is. If it is not clear, restate it in your own words or ask the board member to clarify it for you. However, do not haggle about minor elements.

### 10) Reply promptly but not hastily

A common entry on oral board rating sheets is "candidate responded readily," or "candidate hesitated in replies." Respond as promptly and quickly as you can, but do not jump to a hasty, ill-considered answer.

### 11) Do not be peremptory in your answers

A brief answer is proper – but do not fire your answer back. That is a losing game from your point of view. The board member can probably ask questions much faster than you can answer them.

### 12) Do not try to create the answer you think the board member wants

He is interested in what kind of mind you have and how it works – not in playing games. Furthermore, he can usually spot this practice and will actually grade you down on it.

### 13) Do not switch sides in your reply merely to agree with a board member

Frequently, a member will take a contrary position merely to draw you out and to see if you are willing and able to defend your point of view. Do not start a debate, yet do not surrender a good position. If a position is worth taking, it is worth defending.

### 14) Do not be afraid to admit an error in judgment if you are shown to be wrong

The board knows that you are forced to reply without any opportunity for careful consideration. Your answer may be demonstrably wrong. If so, admit it and get on with the interview.

### 15) Do not dwell at length on your present job

The opening question may relate to your present assignment. Answer the question but do not go into an extended discussion. You are being examined for a *new* job, not your present one. As a matter of fact, try to phrase ALL your answers in terms of the job for which you are being examined.

*Basis of Rating*

Probably you will forget most of these "do's" and "don'ts" when you walk into the oral interview room. Even remembering them all will not ensure you a passing grade. Perhaps you did not have the qualifications in the first place. But remembering them will help you to put your best foot forward, without treading on the toes of the board members.

Rumor and popular opinion to the contrary notwithstanding, an oral board wants you to make the best appearance possible. They know you are under pressure – but they also want to see how you respond to it as a guide to what your reaction would be under the pressures of the job you seek. They will be influenced by the degree of poise you display, the personal traits you show and the manner in which you respond.


ABOUT THIS BOOK

This book contains tests divided into Examination Sections. Go through each test, answering every question in the margin. We have also attached a sample answer sheet at the back of the book that can be removed and used. At the end of each test look at the answer key and check your answers. On the ones you got wrong, look at the right answer choice and learn. Do not fill in the answers first. Do not memorize the questions and answers, but understand the answer and principles involved. On your test, the questions will likely be different from the samples. Questions are changed and new ones added. If you understand these past questions you should have success with any changes that arise. Tests may consist of several types of questions. We have additional books on each subject should more study be advisable or necessary for you. Finally, the more you study, the better prepared you will be. This book is intended to be the last thing you study before you walk into the examination room. Prior study of relevant texts is also recommended. NLC publishes some of these in our Fundamental Series. Knowledge and good sense are important factors in passing your exam. Good luck also helps. So now study this Passbook, absorb the material contained within and take that knowledge into the examination. Then do your best to pass that exam.

# EXAMINATION SECTION

# EXAMINATION SECTION

## TEST 1

DIRECTIONS: Each question or incomplete statement is followed by several suggested answers or completions. Select the one that BEST answers the question or completes the statement. *PRINT THE LETTER OF THE CORRECT ANSWER IN THE SPACE AT THE RIGHT.*

1. If a defendant wishes neither to admit to nor contest the charge that has been brought against him/her, what is the proper phrase to describe this plea?
    A. Stare decisis
    B. Nolo contendere
    C. Non obstante veredicto
    D. Res Ipsa Loquitur

    1.____

2. If an attorney is attempting to prove that a contract signed by his client is invalid, what condition must be met to support this claim?
    A. The client was under the influence at the time of signing.
    B. The client's first name was misspelled on the contract.
    C. The client was a minor at the time of contract signing.
    D. There was no witness to the contract signing.

    2.____

3. When asked to file an appeal from a final order of the trial court, what should be the FIRST step taken?
    A. Obtain transcripts from the trial
    B. Prepare the notice of appeal for filing
    C. Collect the trial exhibits into an appellate record
    D. Determine the date in which the initial filing with the appeals court must be made

    3.____

4. An attorney states that there is a case-on-point supporting his argument. This case law must be followed according to what principle?
    A. Stare decisis
    B. Nolo contendere
    C. Non obstante veredicto
    D. Res Ipsa Loquitur

    4.____

5. If neighboring property owners dispute whether or not a written and recorded easement grant certain rights, what action should be filed to settle this dispute?
    A. A criminal action
    B. A negligence action
    C. A declaratory judgment action
    D. An action for monetary damages

    5.____

6. If a lawsuit has been filed and the summons has been delivered to the defendant, what happens if the defendant fails to file an answer within the time frame set by the court?
    A. The suit will move to trial.
    B. The defendant will be held in contempt of court.
    C. The clerk of courts will contact the defendant.
    D. The counsel of the plaintiff may file a motion for default judgment.

    6.____

7. If you are assigned to give notice to a witness of a deposition, what means is acceptable to give this notice?
   A. Written notice by mail
   B. Written notice by e-mail
   C. Verbal notice over the phone
   D. Verbal notice face-to-face

8. If a judge enters a judgment and awards damages to a client who incurred no financial losses as a result of the conduct underlying the case, what type of damages has this judge awarded?
   A. Nominal damages
   B. Punitive damages
   C. Compensatory damages
   D. Arbitrary damages

9. If an attorney asks an assistant to check the validity of a case he cites in his/her brief, after the case has been Shepardized, which of the following case histories indicate that the case is no longer good law?
   A. The case was vacated on appeal.
   B. The case was distinguished on appeal.
   C. The case was followed but distinguished.
   D. The appellate court opinion vacating the case was overturned.

10. Which of the following is not part of discovery?
    A. Admissions
    B. Motion to compel
    C. Motion to dismiss
    D. Request for production of documents

11. Which of the following is a body of law developed from custom or judicial decisions in English and U.S. courts and not attributable to a legislature?
    A. Civil law
    B. Common law
    C. Criminal law
    D. Statutory law

12. What type of court decision furnishes an example or authority for deciding subsequent cases in which identical or similar facts are presented?
    A. An analogy
    B. A precedent
    C. Stare decisis
    D. A common law

13. A(n) _____ is a written law enacted by a legislature under its constitutional law-making authority.
    A. Statute
    B. Court's opinion
    C. Constitutional provision
    D. Administrative regulation

14. Which of the following is a body of law created by government agencies, in the form of rules, regulations, orders and decisions, used to carry out their duties and responsibilities?
    A. Case law
    B. Statutory law
    C. Administrative law
    D. Constitutional law

15. A remedy based on rules of fairness, justice, and honesty is termed 15.____
    A. remedy at law              B. civil law remedy
    C. remedy in equity           D. common law remedy

16. Of the three branches of federal government, what branch is responsible 16.____
    for making statutory law?
    A. Judicial       B. Executive      C. Legislative     D. Administrative

17. Which of the following is an order, rule, or law enacted by a municipal or 17.____
    county government to govern a local matter unaddressed by state or federal
    legislature?
    A. Statute                    B. Ordinance
    C. Court opinion              D. Administrative rule

18. Court of _____ jurisdiction is defined as a state court that can hear a variety 18.____
    of different matters, from civil lawsuits to criminal actions.
    A. limited        B. general        C. global          D. exclusive

19. _____ jurisdiction is defined as jurisdiction that exists when two different 19.____
    courts have the power to hear the same case, such as when a case can be
    heard in either federal or state court.
    A. Global         B. Exclusive      C. Appellate       D. Concurrent

20. Which of the following is the purpose of a complaint? 20.____
    A. To initiate a lawsuit
    B. To dismiss a lawsuit
    C. To request the court to issue an order
    D. To obtain information the other party possesses

21. Motion to _____ is a document filed by either party asking the court to 21.____
    compel the other to comply with a discovery request.
    A. strike                     B. dismiss
    C. compel discovery           D. make more definite and certain

22. Which of the following statements BEST describes the difference between a 22.____
    deposition and an interrogatory?
    A. Interrogatory questions are usually unlimited in number, whereas
       depositions are not.
    B. Depositions are given under oath and interrogatories are not.
    C. Interrogatories are governed by court rules and depositions are not.
    D. Depositions consist of oral questions and interrogatories are written.

23. Which of the following statements is TRUE regarding FRCP 26? 23.____
    A. The discovery process will take longer.
    B. State court rules have been abolished.
    C. Automatic disclosure of relevant information is required.
    D. Depositions, interrogatories, and other discovery tools have been
       eliminated.

24. A motion filed with the court requesting that certain evidence that may be prejudicial, irrelevant, or legally inadmissible not be brought out during trial is termed a motion
    A. in limine
    B. for a new trial
    C. for a directed verdict
    D. for a judgment as a matter of law

24.____

25. _____ is defined as questioning potential jurors to determine if they should serve on the jury for the case at hand.
    A. Voir dire    B. Subpoena    C. Arraignment    D. Interrogatory

25.____

# KEY (CORRECT ANSWERS)

| | | | |
|---|---|---|---|
| 1. | B | 11. | B |
| 2. | C | 12. | B |
| 3. | D | 13. | A |
| 4. | A | 14. | C |
| 5. | C | 15. | C |
| 6. | D | 16. | C |
| 7. | A | 17. | B |
| 8. | A | 18. | B |
| 9. | A | 19. | D |
| 10. | C | 20. | A |

21. C
22. D
23. C
24. A
25. A

# TEST 2

DIRECTIONS: Each question or incomplete statement is followed by several suggested answers or completions. Select the one that BEST answers the question or completes the statement. *PRINT THE LETTER OF THE CORRECT ANSWER IN THE SPACE AT THE RIGHT.*

1. Which of the following statements is TRUE regarding paralegals? 1.____
   Paralegals
   A. may practice law
   B. may not practice law
   C. do only clerical work
   D. must obtain a license to work by the state

2. All of the following duties are within the scope of practice for a law assistant or paralegal preparing a case for trial EXCEPT 2.____
   A. researching issues  B. contacting witnesses
   C. preparing a trial notebook  D. arguing pretrial motions in court

3. Which of the following is defined as the examination of a witness by the attorney who calls the witness to the stand to testify on behalf of the attorney's client? 3.____
   A. Voir dire  B. Direct examination
   C. Cross examination  D. Redirect examination

4. What type of question suggests a desired answer and usually only permitted to be asked of a hostile witness under direct examination? 4.____
   A. Leading  B. Hypothetical
   C. Open-ended  D. Closed-ended

5. If an appellate court decides to uphold the judgment of a trial court, what has the appellate court done to the judgment of the trial court? 5.____
   A. Affirmed  B. Appealed  C. Reversed  D. Overruled

6. The constitutional rights of accused persons taken into custody by law enforcement officials are known as _____ rights. 6.____
   A. Quarles  B. Miranda
   C. Custodial  D. Exclusionary rule

7. The _____ Rule is a rule of criminal procedure under which any evidence obtained in violation of the accused constitutional rights will NOT be admissible in court. 7.____
   A. Miranda  B. Quarles
   C. Admittance  D. Exclusionary

8. What type of damages are awarded to the non-breaching party to a contract for the loss of the bargain? 8.____
   A. Punitive  B. Liquidated
   C. Consequential  D. Compensatory

9.  Which of the following represent the four elements of negligence? Duty, breach,
    A. cause, injury
    B. capacity, injury
    C. capacity, cause
    D. agreement, consideration

10. Substantial evidence, as required to confirm the finding of an administrative agency on judicial review, is
    A. evidence beyond a reasonable doubt
    B. such relevant evidence as a reasonable mind might accept as adequate to support a conclusion
    C. a mere scintilla of evidence
    D. a preponderance of the evidence

11. A(n) _____ is a civil wrong, not arising from a breach of contract, but arising from a breach of legal duty that causes harm or injury to another.
    A. tort    B. felony    C. assault    D. misdemeanor

12. If a jury issues a verdict that $150,000 is awarded to the plaintiff that is reduced to $100,000 due to the conduct of the plaintiff, this reduction is due to
    A. breach of contract
    B. intentional tort
    C. comparative negligence
    D. contributory negligence

13. Which of the following exists when the connection between an act and an injury is strong enough to justify imposing liability as a matter of public policy?
    A. Duty
    B. Cause in fact
    C. Probable cause
    D. Proximate cause

14. All of the following are examples of intentional tort EXCEPT
    A. battery    B. defamation    C. slip and fall    D. trespassing

15. Which of the following is a distinctive mark, motto, device, or emblem that a manufacturer stamps, prints, or otherwise affixes to the goods it produces so they can be identified on the market?
    A. Copyright    B. Trademark    C. Patent    D. Trade name

16. _____ property consist of the products that result from the creative processes of a person such as literary works, artistic works, or computer software.
    A. Real    B. Public    C. Personal    D. Intellectual

17. The government grant that gives an inventory the exclusive right or privilege to make, use, or sell an invention for a limited time is referred to as a(n)
    A. patent    B. copyright    C. trade name    D. trade secret

18. Which of the following would handle grievances against lawyers?
    A. State Bars and Regulatory Departments
    B. State Bar Associations
    C. Judicial Grievance Departments
    D. County Clerks

19. In order for a judge to grant a motion for summary judgment, what conditions must be met?
    A. The defendant fails to answer the complaint.
    B. The facts in the complaint cannot be proven.
    C. No facts exist to prove the guilt of the defendant.
    D. There is no material issue of fact or law that would entitle the respondent to judgment.

20. All of the following are parts of the summons and service process EXCEPT
    A. the answer
    B. the complaint
    C. evidence of service process
    D. a date set by the court to respond to the complaint

21. A paralegal's BEST response to a call from a new client needing immediate legal advice is
    A. "The law is that....."
    B. "You should take the following action....."
    C. "Let me do some research and get back to you."
    D. "I'll inform the attorney and he will get back to you."

22. All of the following would be under the scope of practice for a paralegal EXCEPT
    A. drafting complaints
    B. signing pleadings
    C. interviewing witnesses
    D. assisting in jury selection

23. Any of the following situations could lead to either criminal or civil charges being filed against a person. Of these, which one would MOST likely result in a civil lawsuit?
    A. A physical fight between domestic partners
    B. A customer bouncing a check
    C. A minor stealing a DVD from a store
    D. A DUI accident that resulted in significant property damage

24. A company has filed a motion with the U.S. Patent and Trademark Office to trademark its logo. Until the motion is granted, what symbol should the company use next to their logo?
    A. ®
    B. TM
    C. Either ® or TM is acceptable
    D. No symbol should be used until motion is granted or denied

25. In order to be recoverable, which of the following remedies for breach of contract must be included in the contract?
    A. Equitable relief
    B. Punitive damages
    C. Consequential damages
    D. Attorney fees and costs

## KEY (CORRECT ANSWERS)

| | | | | |
|---|---|---|---|---|
| 1. | B | | 11. | A |
| 2. | D | | 12. | C |
| 3. | B | | 13. | D |
| 4. | A | | 14. | C |
| 5. | A | | 15. | B |
| | | | | |
| 6. | B | | 16. | D |
| 7. | D | | 17. | A |
| 8. | D | | 18. | A |
| 9. | A | | 19. | D |
| 10. | D | | 20. | A |

21. D
22. B
23. B
24. B
25. D

# TEST 3

DIRECTIONS: Each question or incomplete statement is followed by several suggested answers or completions. Select the one that BEST answers the question or completes the statement. *PRINT THE LETTER OF THE CORRECT ANSWER IN THE SPACE AT THE RIGHT.*

1. Which of the following processes refers to the practice of rewriting a previously signed contract in order to clarify and correct the errors?
   A. Recission
   B. Reformation
   C. Redrafting
   D. Renovating

    1._____

2. In what situation would a paralegal inadvertently violate the attorney-client privilege?
   A. Mailing discovery to the opposing counsel
   B. Talking about your day in court in a public place among friends
   C. Talking to the client on the phone while in a crowded elevator
   D. Sending an e-mail to your boss that discusses details of the case and copying co-counsel

    2._____

3. Which of the following refers to the action of a defendant in a civil action wanting to file a claim against the plaintiff?
   A. Cross-claim
   B. Counterclaim
   C. Causal claim
   D. Callous claim

    3._____

4. When researching a legal problem, the main objective is to locate primary (mandatory) authority within your jurisdiction.
   Primary authority would NOT include
   A. legislation
   B. judicial decisions
   C. administrative rules
   D. law revision commission reports

    4._____

5. Which of the following is defined as confidential information?
   A. All information that is obtained directly from the client
   B. Information gathered over the course of a paralegal's career
   C. Only information that is embarrassing or harmful to the client
   D. All information, relating to the representation of a client, regardless of the source

    5._____

6. The duty of confidentiality is an implied duty. What is mean by the term "implied"?
   A. That it is assumed
   B. That it is written down
   C. That it is not written in the contract, but required
   D. That everyone knows about it, but should not be talked about

    6._____

7. Which of the following are sources of confidential information?
   A. Only written information
   B. Only information gathered directly from the client
   C. Private and personal information obtained from people
   D. The client, other people, and sources other than people that are public or private

8. All of the following are examples of confidential information EXCEPT information
   A. that is spoken and cannot be proven
   B. that the client reveals, but is generally known
   C. obtained from family members of the client
   D. that is not at all related to the representation of your client

9. For what time period is the duty of confidentiality in effect?
   A. Forever
   B. Until the death of the client
   C. Until the court closes the case
   D. Until the end of the attorney/client relationship

10. Which of the following is represented by the term "UPL"?
    A. Underpaid Paralegal Legion      B. Understood Paralegal Lessons
    C. Unauthorized Practice of Law    D. Understanding Personal Lawyers

11. UPL has a three-part definition. Number one is "The application of a rule of law". Number two is "to a particular person's fact pattern", and number three is
    A. writing it down               B. being sure of your answer
    C. giving a response or answer   D. telling the lawyer your answer

12. Legislation has been enacted that restricts the practice of law to only licensed attorneys to protect which of the following?
    A. Paralegals      B. Plaintiffs
    C. Defendants      D. The general public

13. Unauthorized practice of law regulations prohibit all of the following EXCEPT
    A. giving legal advice
    B. answering interrogatories
    C. signing legal documents for others
    D. representing others in court

14. Which of the following statements BEST defines the "incidental to" rule?
    A. An exception that allows paralegals to practice law for elderly clients
    B. A federal rule of law that allows courts to use paralegals as law clerks
    C. A rule that states that paralegals can practice law if it is within the course and scope of their job
    D. A rule that allows certain professionals to give some legal advice as part of their jobs (such as realtors)

15. Conduit theory is BEST defined as a
    A. rule of law that allows paralegals to practice construction law
    B. theory that allows paralegals to practice law in real estate closings
    C. federal rule of law that allows states to choose whether or not to allow paralegals to practice law
    D. theory that allows paralegals to pass along legal advice to clients or information given to paralegals by supervising lawyers

16. For what reason are UPL issues difficult to determine when it comes to corporations?
    A. Corporate employees are sometimes exempt from overtime pay.
    B. The internal workings of corporations are hidden from public scrutiny.
    C. Corporations are not "persons" so they cannot use the right of self-representation.
    D. Corporations typically pay paralegals more money so they are expected to do more work, such as given legal advice

17. Which of the following statements is TRUE regarding American Bar Association's Model Rules of Professional Conduct?
    It is
    A. an old, antiquated code of conduct that is seldom used in today's practice
    B. composed of rules that govern lawyers but not paralegals
    C. composed of rules that have been adopted in almost all states
    D. composed of nationally recognized rules of professional responsibility in all fifth states

18. Which of the following statements is TRUE regarding local bar association ethics opinions?
    They are
    A. advisory and persuasive
    B. never published and have no legal effect
    C. binding on all lawyers and paralegals in the states
    D. binding on all lawyers in the territorial jurisdiction of the bar association

19. The term "grandfather clause" is BEST defined as
    A. a rule of law that only applies to those over the age of 65
    B. a clause in a contract that will apply to situations that have passed but not to future situations
    C. the federal rule of law that allows larger companies to employ older Americans without enforcing retirement regulations
    D. an exception that allows an old rule to continue to apply to some situations when a new rule will apply instead to all future situations

20. Which of the following terms BEST defines the term "sunset provision"?
    A. A part of a law that ends at a certain time
    B. A rule of law that pertains to air quality
    C. A provision in a contract that specifies when the contract will end
    D. A federal rule of law that allows states whether or not to invoke daylight savings time

21. The term "title scheme" is BEST defined as
    A. a type of regulatory act that restricts the use of certain titles
    B. the format used by the federal government to give titles to different statutes
    C. the informal but widely used convention for naming new scientific discoveries
    D. the law that prevents improper use of subtitles in movies and television production

22. Which of the following statements is TRUE regarding the American Bar Association?
    It is a(n)
    A. voluntary organization for lawyers
    B. disciplinary authority relied upon by nearly all of the states
    C. mandatory organization for the licensing of lawyers and paralegals
    D. organization that was once very powerful but is now insignificant to practicing attorneys

23. Which of the following is one of the duties that paralegals have in handling client funds?
    A. To annually provide full accounting
    B. To deliver client funds and property within three business days
    C. To keep accurate and complete records of client funds and property
    D. To notify clients the same day that funds or property are received

24. Which of the following would be implicated if a lawyer represents both the husband and wife who are seeking divorce?
    A. Ethical wall doctrine
    B. Conflict of interest rule
    C. Doctrine of open communication
    D. Rule of attorney/client confidentiality

25. Which of the following is the MOST important ethical consideration for those who work as freelance paralegals?
    A. Overbilling
    B. Confidentiality
    C. Conflict of interest
    D. Lack of certification

## KEY (CORRECT ANSWERS)

1. B
2. C
3. B
4. B
5. A

6. C
7. B
8. D
9. A
10. C

11. C
12. D
13. B
14. D
15. D

16. C
17. C
18. A
19. D
20. C

21. A
22. A
23. C
24. B
25. B

# TEST 4

DIRECTIONS: Each question or incomplete statement is followed by several suggested answers or completions. Select the one that BEST answers the question or completes the statement. *PRINT THE LETTER OF THE CORRECT ANSWER IN THE SPACE AT THE RIGHT.*

1. Which of the following must be TRUE in order for the work product doctrine to apply?
Written materials must
    A. be admissions of liability
    B. be admissible as evidence at trial
    C. have been prepared by an attorney
    D. have been prepared in preparation for trial

    1.____

2. The reading of Miranda rights protects the defendant from which of the following?
    A. Double-jeopardy
    B. Unlawful searches
    C. Unlawful seizures
    D. Self-incrimination

    2.____

3. Which of the following is NOT the function of a bill of particulars? To
    A. amplify the pleadings
    B. obtain your adversary's evidence
    C. limit proof at trial
    D. prevent surprise at trial

    3.____

4. Which of the following is meant by the term "forwarding the record"?
    A. Giving the appellee the required copies of appellant briefs
    B. Summarizing the trial transcript to look for errors of procedure
    C. Highlighting the allegations of error that were committed by the trial court
    D. Ordering from the court reporter the transcript of the proceeding not already on file

    4.____

5. Which of the following is the defense that involves arguing that the plaintiff's harm was an unforeseen event?
    A. Strict liability
    B. Superseding event
    C. Assumption of risk
    D. Comparative negligence

    5.____

6. _____ is the doctrine that makes a defendant liable even if the defendant is without fault.
    A. Strict liability
    B. Assumption of risk
    C. Contributory negligence
    D. Comparative negligence

    6.____

7. A covenant is BEST defined as a(n)
    A. condition precedent
    B. condition subsequent
    C. incomplete performance
    D. promise or agreement

    7.____

8. An unconscionable contract is also referred to as which of the following?
    A. Executed contract
    B. Contract of adhesion
    C. Statute of frauds contract
    D. Contract of unfavorability

    8.____

9. Which of the following is considered to be *prima facie* evidence of a partnership?
Sharing of
   A. profits
   B. authority
   C. management
   D. expenses

10. Which of the following BEST defines a limited liability company?
    A. An incorporated partnership
    B. An unincorporated partnership
    C. An incorporated business entity
    D. An unincorporated business entity

11. In order to be patented, an invention must be all of the following EXCEPT
    A. novel    B. useful    C. credible    D. nonobvious

12. For what time period does copyright protection last?
The life-span of the
    A. author
    B. author plus 10 years
    C. author plus 50 years
    D. author plus 70 years

13. All of the following are required for a will to be valid EXCEPT the
    A. will must be in writing
    B. testator must sign the will
    C. will must be prepared by an attorney
    D. testator must have testamentary capacity

14. Which of the following would be able to change a previously executed will?
    A. Codicil    B. Attestation    C. Abatement    D. Revocation

15. All of the following courts make precedent EXCEPT
    A. state supreme courts
    B. circuit courts of appeals
    C. intermediate appellate courts
    D. general-jurisdiction trial courts

16. All of the following are forms of alternative dispute resolution EXCEPT
    A. litigation    B. mini-trials    C. mediation    D. arbitration

17. Which of the following statements is TRUE regarding the delegation doctrine?
    A. A federal agency only has the power that has been delegated to it by the director of the agency.
    B. A state agency only has the power that its counterpart federal agency has delegated to it.
    C. Employees of federal agencies only have the power that their agency supervisors have delegated to them.
    D. Federal and state agencies only have the power that has been delegated to them by their authorizing legislation or executive orders.

18. A federal agency has all of the following delegated legislative powers EXCEPT
    A. statements of policy
    B. substantive rule making
    C. interpretive rule making
    D. adjudicate determinations

19. What piece of legislation allows the public to request access to most documents in the possession of federal agencies?
    A. Privacy Act
    B. Equal Access to Justice Act
    C. Freedom of Information Act
    D. Government in the Sunshine Act

    19._____

20. If a grand jury believes there is sufficient evidence to hold the accused for trial, it issues a(n)
    A. indictment
    B. arraignment
    C. default judgment
    D. affirmative judgment

    20._____

21. In order to prove a pattern of racketeering, the government must show that the defendant committed how many acts within what time frame? _____ acts within a _____-year period.
    A. two; 5
    B. two; 10
    C. three; 5
    D. three; 10

    21._____

22. The prohibition against cruel and unusual punishment is found in which Constitutional Amendment?
    A. 1st
    B. 4th
    C. 5th
    D. 8th

    22._____

23. All of the following are a type of co-ownership EXCEPT
    A. joint tenancy
    B. tenancy in common
    C. tenancy by the entirety
    D. tenancy by the reversion

    23._____

24. Community property states require that upon the death of one spouse, the co-spouse is entitled to which of the following? _____ property of the deceased spouse.
    A. All of the
    B. Half of the
    C. All of the marital
    D. Half of the marital

    24._____

25. Which of the following is defined as taking title to someone else's real estate by treating it as your own for the required period of time and under the other required statutory requirements?
    A. Quiet title
    B. Quitclaim deed
    C. Squatter's rights
    D. Adverse possession

    25._____

## KEY (CORRECT ANSWERS)

| | | | |
|---|---|---|---|
| 1. | C | 11. | C |
| 2. | D | 12. | D |
| 3. | A | 13. | C |
| 4. | D | 14. | A |
| 5. | B | 15. | D |
| 6. | A | 16. | A |
| 7. | D | 17. | D |
| 8. | B | 18. | D |
| 9. | A | 19. | C |
| 10. | C | 20. | A |

21. B
22. D
23. D
24. D
25. D

# EXAMINATION SECTION
# TEST 1

DIRECTIONS: Each question or incomplete statement is followed by several suggested answers or completions. Select the one that BEST answers the question or completes the statement. *PRINT THE LETTER OF THE CORRECT ANSWER IN THE SPACE AT THE RIGHT.*

Questions 1-4.

DIRECTIONS: Questions 1 through 4 are to be answered on the basis of the following passage.

Those engaged in the exercise of First Amendment rights by pickets, marches, parades, and open-air assemblies are not exempted from obeying valid local traffic ordinances. In a recent pronouncement, Mr. Justice Baxter, speaking for the Supreme Court, wrote:

*The rights of free speech and assembly, while fundamental to our democratic society, still do not mean that everyone with opinions or beliefs to express may address a group at any public place and at any time. The constitutional guarantee of liberty implies the existence of an organized society maintaining public order, without which liberty itself would be lost in the excesses of anarchy. The control of travel on the streets is a clear example of governmental responsibility to insure this necessary order. A restriction in that relation, designed to promote the public convenience in the interest of all, and not susceptible to abuses of discriminatory application, cannot be disregarded by the attempted exercise of some civil rights which, in other circumstances, would be entitled to protection. One would not be justified in ignoring the familiar red light because this was thought to be a means of social protest. Governmental authorities have the duty and responsibility to keep their streets open and available for movement. A group of demonstrators could not insist upon the right to cordon off a street, or entrance to a public or private building, and allow no one to pass who did not agree to listen to their exhortations.*

1. Which of the following statements BEST reflects Mr. Justice Baxter's view of the relationship between liberty and public order?

    A. Public order cannot exist without liberty.
    B. Liberty cannot exist without public order.
    C. The existence of liberty undermines the existence of public order.
    D. The maintenance of public order insures the existence of liberty.

1.____

2. According to the above passage, local traffic ordinances result from

    A. governmental limitations on individual liberty
    B. governmental responsibility to insure public order
    C. majority rule as determined by democratic procedures
    D. restrictions on expression of dissent

2.____

3. The foregoing passage suggests that government would be acting IMPROPERLY if a local traffic ordinance

    A. was enforced in a discriminatory manner
    B. resulted in public inconvenience

3.____

C. violated the right of free speech and assembly
D. was not essential to public order

4. Of the following, the MOST appropriate title for the above passage is:  4._____

   A. THE RIGHTS OF FREE SPEECH AND ASSEMBLY
   B. ENFORCEMENT OF LOCAL TRAFFIC ORDINANCES
   C. FIRST AMENDMENT RIGHTS AND LOCAL TRAFFIC ORDINANCES
   D. LIBERTY AND ANARCHY

Questions 5-8.

DIRECTIONS: Questions 5 through 8 are to be answered on the basis of the following passage.

*On November 8, 1976, the Supreme Court refused to block the payment of Medicaid funds for elective abortions. The Court's action means that a new Federal statute that bars the use of Federal funds for abortions unless abortion is necessary to save the life of the mother will not go into effect for many months, if at all.*

*A Federal District Court in Brooklyn ruled the following month that the statute was unconstitutional and ordered that Federal reimbursement for the costs of abortions continue on the same basis as reimbursements for the costs of pregnancy and childbirth-related services.*

*Technically, what the Court did today was to deny a request by Senator Howard Ramsdell and others for a stay blocking enforcement of the District Court order pending appeal. The Court's action was a victory for New York City. The City's Health and Hospitals Corporation initiated one of the two lawsuits challenging the new statute that led to the District Court's decision. The Corporation also opposed the request for a Supreme Court stay of that decision, telling the Court in a memorandum that a stay would subject the Corporation to a grave and irreparable injury."*

5. According to the above passage, it would be CORRECT to state that the Health and Hospitals Corporation  5._____

   A. joined Senator Ramsdell in his request for a stay
   B. opposed the statute which limited reimbursement for the cost of abortions
   C. claimed that it would experience a loss if the District Court order was enforced
   D. appealed the District Court decision

6. The above passage indicates that the Supreme Court acted in DIRECT response to  6._____

   A. a lawsuit initiated by the Health and Hospitals Corporation
   B. a ruling by a Federal District Court
   C. a request for a stay
   D. the passage of a new Federal statute

7. According to the above passage, it would be CORRECT to state that the Supreme Court  7._____

   A. blocked enforcement of the District Court order
   B. refused a request for a stay to block enforcement of the Federal statute
   C. ruled that the new Federal statute was unconstitutional
   D. permitted payment of Federal funds for abortion to continue

8. Following are three statements concerning abortion that might be correct:
    I. Abortion costs are no longer to be Federally reimbursed on the same basis as those for pregnancy and childbirth
    II. Federal funds have not been available for abortions except to save the life of the mother
    III. Medicaid has paid for elective abortions in the past

   According to the passage given above, which of the following CORRECTLY classifies the above statements into those that are true and those that are not true?

   A. I is true, but II and III are not.
   B. I and III are true, but II is not.
   C. I and II are true, but III is not.
   D. III is true, but I and II are not.

   8.____

9. A legal memorandum will often include the following six sections:
    I. Conclusions
    II. Issues
    III. Analysis
    IV. Facts
    V. Unknowns
    VI. Counter-analysis

   Which of the following choices lists these sections in the sequence that is generally MOST appropriate for a legal memorandum?

   A. III, VI, IV, V, II, I       B. IV, II, III, VI, I, V
   C. V, II, IV, III, VI, I       D. II, IV, V, III, I, VI

   9.____

Questions 10-13.

DIRECTIONS: Questions 10 through 13 consist of two sentences each. The sentences deal with the use of court opinions and cases in the writing of legal memoranda. Select answer
   A. if only sentence I is correct
   B. if only sentence II is correct
   C. if both sentences are correct
   D. if neither sentence is correct

10. I. State the issues in the case as narrowly and precisely as possible.
    II. Quote frequently and at great length from the court opinions.

    10.____

11. I. Describe briefly the issues in the case that are not related to your problem.
    II. Do not mention discrepancies between the facts of the case and the facts of your problem.

    11.____

12. I. Do not refer to the holding or ruling in the case if it is harmful to your client.
    II. If the holding or ruling in the case is beneficial to your client, try to show that the facts of your problem are analogous to the facts of the case.

    12.____

13.  I. After stating your position concerning the issues and facts, present the opposite viewpoint as effectively as you can.
    II. Avoid stating your own opinions or conclusions concerning the applicability of the case.

14. Column V lists four publications in the legal field. Column W contains descriptions of basic subject matter of legal publications.
Select the one of the following choices which BEST matches the publications in Column V with the subject matter in Column W.

    | Column V | Column W |
    |---|---|
    | I. Harvard Law Review | 1. Law |
    | II. Supreme Court Reporter | 2. Commentary on law |
    | III. McKinney's Consolidated Laws of New York | 3. Combination of law and commentary |
    | IV. The Criminal Law Reporter | |

    A. I-3; II-1; III-2; IV-3
    B. I-2; II-3; III-2; IV-3
    C. I-2; II-1; III-3; IV-3
    D. I-2; II-3; III-3; IV-1

15. Tickler systems are used in many legal offices for scheduling and calendar control. Of the following, the LEAST common use of a tickler system is to

    A. keep papers filed in such a way that they may easily be retrieved
    B. arrange for the appearance of witnesses when they will be needed
    C. remind lawyers when certain papers are due
    D. arrange for the gathering of certain types of evidence

# KEY (CORRECT ANSWERS)

1. B
2. B
3. A
4. C
5. B

6. C
7. D
8. D
9. B
10. A

11. D
12. B
13. A
14. C
15. A

# TEST 2

DIRECTIONS: Each question or incomplete statement is followed by several suggested answers or completions. Select the one that BEST answers the question or completes the statement. *PRINT THE LETTER OF THE CORRECT ANSWER IN THE SPACE AT THE RIGHT.*

1. Studying the legislative history of a statute by reading the transcript of the hearings that were held on that subject is useful to the legal researcher PRIMARILY because it

    A. is informative of the manner in which laws are enacted
    B. helps him to understand the intent of the statute
    C. provides leads to statutes on the same subject
    D. clarifies the meaning of other statutes

2. Following are three statements concerning legal research that might be correct:
    I. The researcher may begin with a particular premise and, in researching it, may discover an entirely new approach to the problem
    II. When the researcher has located a relevant statute, it is not necessary to read court opinions interpreting or applying this statute
    III. A statute which is related to, but not the same as, the point being researched may have notes which will refer the researcher to more relevant cases

    Which of the following ACCURATELY classifies the above statements into those which are correct and those which are not?

    A. II and III are correct, but I is not.
    B. I and III are correct, but II is not.
    C. I and II are correct, but III is not.
    D. I, II, and III are all correct.

3. Of the following, the FIRST action a legal researcher should take in order to locate the laws relevant to a case is to

    A. search the index of a law book
    B. read statutes on similar subjects to discover pertinent annotations
    C. read a legal digest to become familiar with the law on the subject
    D. prepare a list of descriptive words applicable to the facts of the case

4. Which of the following is the BEST source for a legal researcher to consult in order to find historical data, cross-references, and case excerpts on cases, statutes, and regulations?

    A. Annotations       B. Digests
    C. Hornbooks         D. Casebooks

Questions 5-8.

DIRECTIONS: Each of Questions 5 through 8 contains two sentences concerning criminal law. Some of the sentences contain errors in English grammar or usage. A sentence does not contain an error simply because it could be written in a different manner. For each question, choose answer
    A. if only sentence I is correct
    B. if only sentence II is correct
    C. if both sentences are correct
    D. if neither sentence is correct

5.   I. Limiting the term *property* to tangible property, in the criminal mischief setting, accords with prior case law holding that only tangible property came within the purview of the offense of malicious mischief.
    II. Thus, a person who intentionally destroys the property of another, but under an honest belief that he has title to such property, cannot be convicted of criminal mischief under the Revised Penal Law.

6.   I. Very early in it's history, New York enacted statutes from time to time punishing, either as a felony or as a misdemeanor, malicious injuries to various kinds of property: piers, booms, dams, bridges, etc.
    II. The application of the statute is necessarily restricted to trespassory takings with larcenous intent: namely with intent permanently or virtually permanently to *appropriate* property or *deprive* the owner of its use.

7.   I. Since the former Penal Law did not define the instruments of forgery in a general fashion, its crime of forgery was held to be narrower than the common law offense in this respect and to embrace only those instruments explicitly specified in the substantive provisions.
    II. After entering the barn through an open door for the purpose of stealing, it was closed by the defendants.

8.   I. The use of fire or explosives to destroy tangible property is proscribed by the criminal mischief provisions of the Revised Penal Law.
    II. The defendant's taking of a taxicab for the immediate purpose of affecting his escape did not constitute grand larceny

Questions 9-13.

DIRECTIONS:   Questions 9 through 13 are to be answered SOLELY on the basis of the following passage.

*The law is quite clear that evidence obtained in violation of Section 605 of the Federal Communications Act is not admissible in federal court. However, the law as to the admissibility of evidence in state court is far from clear. Had the Supreme Court of the United States made the wiretap exclusionary rule applicable to the states, such confusion would not exist.*

*In the case of Alton v. Texas, the Supreme Court was called upon to determine whether wiretapping by state and local officers came within the proscription of the federal statute and, if so, whether Section 605 required the same remedies for its vindication in state courts. In answer to the first question, Mr. Justice Minton, speaking for the court, flatly stated that Section 605 made it a federal crime for anyone to intercept telephone messages and divulge what he learned. The court went on to say that a state officer who testified in state court concerning the existence, contents, substance, purport, effect or meaning of an intercepted conversation violated the federal law and committed a criminal act. In regard to the second question, however, the Supreme Court felt constrained by due regard for federal-state relations to answer in the negative. Mr. Justice Minton stated that the court would not presume, in the absence of a clear manifestation of congressional intent, that Congress intended to supersede state rules of evidence.*

*Because the Supreme Court refused to apply the exclusionary rule to wiretap evidence that was being used in state courts, the states respectively made this decision for themselves. According to hearings held before a congressional committee in 1975, six states authorize wiretapping by statute, 33 states impose total bans on wiretapping, and 11 states have no definite statute on the subject. For examples of extremes, a statute in Pennsylvania will be compared with a statute in New York.*

*The Pennsylvania statute provides that no communications by telephone or telegraph can be intercepted without permission of both parties. It also specifically prohibits such interception by public officials and provides that evidence obtained cannot be used in court.*

*The lawmakers in New York, recognizing the need for legal wiretapping, authorized wiretapping by statute. A New York law authorizes the issuance of an ex parte order upon oath or affirmation for limited wiretapping. The aim of the New York law is to allow court-ordered wiretapping and to encourage the testimony of state officers concerning such wiretapping in court. The New York law was found to be constitutional by the New York State Supreme Court in 1975. Other states, including Oregon, Maryland, Nevada, and Massachusetts, enacted similar laws which authorize court-ordered wiretapping.*

*To add to this legal disarray, the vast majority of the states, including New Jersey and New York, permit wiretapping evidence to be received in court even though obtained in violation of the state laws and of Section 605 of the Federal act. However, some states such as Rhode Island have enacted statutory exclusionary rules which provide that illegally procured wiretap evidence is incompetent in civil as well as criminal actions.*

9. According to the above passage, a state officer who testifies in New York State court concerning the contents of a conversation he overheard through a court-ordered wiretap is in violation of _____ law.

    A. state law but not federal
    B. federal law but not state
    C. federal law and state
    D. neither federal nor state

10. According to the above passage, which of the following statements concerning states statutes on wiretapping is CORRECT?

    A. The number of states that impose total bans on wiretapping is three times as great as the number of states with no definite statute on wiretapping.
    B. The number of states having no definite statute on wiretapping is more than twice the number of states authorizing wiretapping.
    C. The number of states which authorize wiretapping by statute and the number of states having no definite statute on wiretapping exceed the number of states imposing total bans on wiretapping.
    D. More states authorize wiretapping by statute than impose total bans on wiretapping.

11. Following are three statements concerning wiretapping that might be valid:
    I. In Pennsylvania, only public officials may legally intercept telephone communications
    II. In Rhode Island, evidence obtained through an illegal wiretap is incompetent in criminal, but not civil, actions
    III. Neither Massachusetts nor Pennsylvania authorizes wiretapping by public officials

    According to the above passage, which of the following CORRECTLY classifies these statements into those that are valid and those that are not?

    A. I is valid, but II and III are not.
    B. II is valid, but I and III are not.
    C. II and III are valid, but I is not.
    D. None of the statements is valid.

12. According to the foregoing passage, evidence obtained in violation of Section 605 of the Federal Communications Act is inadmissible in

    A. federal court but not in any state courts
    B. federal court and all state courts
    C. all state courts but not in federal court
    D. federal court and some state courts

13. In regard to state rules of evidence, Mr. Justice Minton expressed the Court's opinion that Congress

    A. intended to supersede state rules of evidence, as manifested by Section 605 of the Federal Communications Act
    B. assumed that federal statutes would govern state rules of evidence in all wiretap cases
    C. left unclear whether it intended to supersede state rules of evidence
    D. precluded itself from superseding state rules of evidence through its regard for federal-state relations

14. You begin to ask follow-up questions of a witness who has given a statement. The witness starts to digress before answering an important question satisfactorily.
    In this situation, the BEST of the following steps is to

    A. guide the interview by suggesting answers to questions as they are asked
    B. ask questions which can be answered only with a simple *yes* or *no*
    C. construct questions as precisely as possible
    D. tell the witness to keep his answers brief

15. During an interview with a client, you have occasion to refer to a matter which is described in the legal profession by a technical term.
    Of the following, it would generally be MOST appropriate for you to

    A. discuss the underlying legal concept in detail
    B. avoid the subject since it is too complicated
    C. ask the client if he is familiar with the technical term
    D. describe the matter in everyday language

## KEY (CORRECT ANSWERS)

1. B
2. B
3. D
4. A
5. C

6. B
7. A
8. A
9. B
10. A

11. D
12. D
13. C
14. C
15. D

# EXAMINATION SECTION
# TEST 1

DIRECTIONS: Each question or incomplete statement is followed by several suggested answers or completions. Select the one that BEST answers the question or completes the statement. *PRINT THE LETTER OF THE CORRECT ANSWER IN THE SPACE AT THE RIGHT.*

Questions 1-4.

DIRECTIONS: Questions 1 through 4 consist of sentences concerning criminal law. Some of the sentences contain errors in English grammar or usage, punctuation, spelling or capitalization. A sentence does not contain an error simply because it could be written in a different manner. Choose answer
    A.  if the sentence contains an error in English grammar or usage
    B.  if the sentence contains an error in punctuation
    C.  if the sentence contains an error in spelling or capitalization
    D.  if the sentence does not contain any errors

1. The severity of the sentence prescribed by contemporary statutes - including both the former and the revised New York Penal Laws - do not depend on what crime was intended by the offender.    1._____

2. It is generally recognized that two defects in the early law of attempt played a part in the birth of burglary: (1) immunity from prosecution for conduct short of the last act before completion of the crime, and (2) the relatively minor penalty imposed for an attempt (it being a common law misdemeanor) vis-a-vis the completed offense.    2._____

3. The first sentence of the statute is applicable to employees who enter their place of employment, invited guests, and all other persons who have an express or implied license or privilege to enter the premises.    3._____

4. Contemporary criminal codes in the United States generally divide burglary into various degrees, differentiating the categories according to place, time and other attendent circumstances.    4._____

Questions 5-8.

DIRECTIONS: Questions 5 through 8 are to be answered SOLELY on the basis of the following passage.

*The difficulty experienced in determining which party has the burden of proving payment or non-payment is due largely to a tack of consistency between the rules of pleading and the rules of proof. In some cases, a plaintiff is obligated by a rule of pleading to allege non-payment on his complaint, yet is not obligated to prove non-payment on the trial. An action upon a contract for the payment of money will serve as an illustration. In such a case, the plaintiff must allege non-payment in his complaint, but the burden of proving payment on the trial is upon the defendant. An important and frequently cited case on this problem is Conkling v. Weatherwax. In that case, the action was brought to establish and enforce a legacy as a lien upon real property. The defendant alleged in her answer that the legacy had been paid. There was no witness competent to testify for the plaintiff to show that the legacy had not* been paid. Therefore, the question of the burden of proof became of primary importance since, if the plaintiff had the burden of proving non-payment, she must fail in her action; whereas, if the burden of proof was on the defendant to prove payment, the plaintiff might win. The Court of Appeals held that the burden of proof was on the plaintiff. In the course of his opinion, Judge Vann attempted to harmonize the conflicting cases on this subject, and for that purpose formulated three rules. These rules have been construed and applied to numerous subsequent cases. As so construed and applied, these may be summarized as follows:

Rule 1: In an action upon a contract for the payment of money only, where the complaint does not allege a balance due over and above all payments made, the plaintiff must allege nonpayment in his complaint, but the burden of proving payment is upon the defendant. In such a case, payment is an affirmative defense which the defendant must plead in his answer. If the defendant fails to plead payment, but pleads a general denial instead, he will not be permitted to introduce evidence of payment.

Rule 2: Where the complaint sets forth a balance in excess of all payments, owing to the structure of the pleading, burden is upon the plaintiff to prove his allegation. In this case, the defendant is not required to plead payment as a defense in his answer but may introduce evidence of payment under a general denial.

Rule 3: When the action is not upon contract for the payment of money, but is upon an obligation created by operation of law, or is for the enforcement of a lien where non-payment of the amount secured is part of the cause of action, it is necessary both to allege and prove the fact of nonpayment.

5. In the above passage, the case of Conkling v. Weatherwax was cited PRIMARILY to illustrate

    A. a case where the burden of proof was on the defendant to prove payment
    B. how the question of the burden of proof can affect the outcome of a case
    C. the effect of a legacy as a lien upon real property
    D. how conflicting cases concerning the burden of proof were harmonized

6. According to the above passage, the pleading of payment is a defense in

    A. Rule 1, but not Rules 2 and 3
    B. Rule 2, but not Rules 1 and 3
    C. Rules 1 and 3, but not Rule 2
    D. Rules 2 and 3, but not Rule 1

7. The facts in Conkling v. Weatherwax closely resemble the conditions described in Rule

    A. 1
    B. 2
    C. 3
    D. none of the rules

8. The major topic of the above passage may BEST be described as

    A. determining the ownership of property
    B. providing a legal definition
    C. placing the burden of proof
    D. formulating rules for deciding cases

Questions 9-12.

DIRECTIONS: Questions 9 through 12 consist of six sentences which can be arranged in a logical sequence. For each question, select the choice which places the numbered sentences in the MOST logical sequence.

9.  I. The burden of proof as to each issue is determined before trial and remains upon the same party throughout the trial.
    II. The jury is at liberty to believe one witness testimony as against a number of contradictory witnesses.
    III. In a civil case, the party bearing the burden of proof is required to prove his contention by a fair preponderance of the evidence.
    IV. However, it must be noted that a fair preponderance of evidence does not necessarily mean a greater number of witnesses.
    V. The burden of proof is the burden which rests upon one of the parties to an action to persuade the trier of the facts, generally the jury, that a proposition he asserts is true.
    VI. If the evidence is equally balanced, or if it leaves the jury in such doubt as to be unable to decide the controversy either way, judgment must be given against the party upon whom the burden of proof rests.

    The CORRECT sequence is:

    A. III, II, V, IV, I, VI
    B. I, II, VI, V, III, IV
    C. III, IV, V, I, II, VI
    D. V, I, III, VI, IV, II

10. I. If a parent is without assets and is unemployed, he cannot be convicted of the crime of non-support of a child.
    II. The term *sufficient ability* has been held to mean sufficient financial ability.
    III. It does not matter if his unemployment is by choice or unavoidable circumstances.
    IV. If he fails to take any steps at all, he may be liable to prosecution for endangering the welfare of a child.
    V. Under the penal law, a parent is responsible for the support of his minor child only if the parent is of sufficient ability.
    VI. An indigent parent may meet his obligation by borrowing money or by seeking aid under the provisions of the Social Welfare Law.

    The CORRECT sequence is:

    A. VI, I, V, III, II, IV
    B. I, III, V, II, IV, VI
    C. V, II, I, III, VI, IV
    D. I, VI, IV, V, II, III

11.
  I. Consider, for example, the case of a rabble rouser who urges a group of twenty people to go out and break the windows of a nearby factory.
  II. Therefore, the law fills the indicated gap with the crime of *inciting to riot*.
  III. A person is considered guilty of inciting to riot when he urges ten or more persons to engage in tumultuous and violent conduct of a kind likely to create public alarm.
  IV. However, if he has not obtained the cooperation of at least four people, he cannot be charged with unlawful assembly.
  V. The charge of inciting to riot was added to the law to cover types of conduct which cannot be classified as either the crime of *riot* or the crime of *unlawful* assembly.
  VI. If he acquires the acquiescence of at least four of them, he is guilty of unlawful assembly even if the project does not materialize.

  The CORRECT sequence is:
  A. III, V, I, VI, IV, II
  B. V, I, IV, VI, II, III
  C. III, IV, I, V, II, VI
  D. V, I, IV, VI, III, II

12.
  I. If, however, the rebuttal evidence presents an issue of credibility, it is for the jury to determine whether the presumption has, in fact, been destroyed.
  II. Once sufficient evidence to the contrary is introduced, the presumption disappears from the trial.
  III. The effect of a presumption is to place the burden upon the adversary to come forward with evidence to rebut the presumption.
  IV. When a presumption is overcome and ceases to exist in the case, the fact or facts which gave rise to the presumption still remain.
  V. Whether a presumption has been overcome is ordinarily a question for the court.
  VI. Such information may furnish a basis for a logical inference.

  The CORRECT sequence is:
  A. IV, VI, II, V, I, III
  B. III, II, V, I, IV, VI
  C. V, III, VI, IV, II, I
  D. V, IV, I, II, VI, III

13. In order to obtain an accurate statement from a person who has witnessed a crime, it is BEST to question the witness

  A. as soon as possible after the crime was committed
  B. after the witness has discussed the crime with other witnesses
  C. after the witness has had sufficient time to reflect on events and formulate a logical statement
  D. after the witness has been advised that he is obligated to tell the whole truth

14. A young woman was stabbed in the hand in her home by her estranged boyfriend. Her mother and two sisters were at home at the time.
  Of the following, it would generally be BEST to interview the young woman in the presence of

  A. her mother only
  B. all members of her immediate family
  C. members of the family who actually observed the crime
  D. the official authorities

15. The one of the following which is NOT effective in obtaining complete testimony from a witness during an interview is to       15.____
    A. ask questions in chronological order
    B. permit the witness to structure the interview
    C. make sure you fully understand the response to each question
    D. review questions to be asked beforehand

---

## KEY (CORRECT ANSWERS)

| | | | |
|---|---|---|---|
| 1. | A | 6. | A |
| 2. | D | 7. | C |
| 3. | D | 8. | C |
| 4. | C | 9. | D |
| 5. | B | 10. | C |

11. A
12. B
13. A
14. D
15. B

---

# TEST 2

DIRECTIONS: Each question or incomplete statement is followed by several suggested answers or completions. Select the one that BEST answers the question or completes the statement. *PRINT THE LETTER OF THE CORRECT ANSWER IN THE SPACE AT THE RIGHT.*

1. You are conducting an initial interview with a witness who expresses reluctance, even hostility, to being questioned. You feel it would be helpful to take some notes during the interview.
   In this situation, it would be BEST to

   A. put off note-taking until a follow-up interview and concentrate on establishing rapport with the witness
   B. explain the necessity of note-taking and proceed to take notes during the interview
   C. make notes from memory after the witness has left
   D. take notes, but as unobtrusively as possible

   1.____

2. An assistant is starting an interview with an elderly man who was the victim of a robbery. The man begins by mentioning his minor aches and pains. The aide immediately changes the subject to the robbery.
   This action by the aide should GENERALLY be considered

   A. *proper* chiefly because it speeds up the interviewing process
   B. *improper* chiefly because the man is likely to become confused as to what information is really important
   C. *proper* chiefly because the man is likely to be impressed with the aide's interest in the crime
   D. *improper* chiefly because an opportunity for gaining pertinent information may be lost

   2.____

3. You are interviewing the owner of a stolen car about facts relating to the robbery. After completing his statement, the car owner suddenly states that some of the details he has just related are not correct. You realize that this change might be significant.
   Of the following, it would be BEST for you to

   A. ask the owner what other details he may have given incorrectly
   B. make a note of the discrepancy for discussion at a later date
   C. repeat your questioning on the details that were misstated until you have covered that area completely
   D. explain to the owner that because of his change of testimony, you will have to repeat the entire interview

   3.____

4. You are interviewing a client who has just been assaulted. He has trouble collecting his thoughts and telling his story coherently.
   Which of the following represents the MOST effective method of questioning under these circumstances?

   A. Ask questions which structure the client's story chronologically into units, each with a beginning, middle, and end.
   B. Ask several questions at a time to structure the interview.

   4.____

C. Ask open-ended questions which allow the client to respond in a variety of ways.
D. Begin the interview with several detailed questions in order to focus the client's attention on the situation.

5. Following are two statements that might be correct concerning the relationship with clients:
   I. When practical the client should be encouraged to take some steps on his own behalf to aid the office in handling his case
   II. The client should be told what steps the office proposes to take on his behalf

   Which of the following CORRECTLY classifies the above statements?

   A. Statement I is generally correct, but Statement II is not.
   B. Statement II is generally correct, but Statement I is not.
   C. Both statements are generally correct.
   D. Neither statement is generally correct.

6. You are in the District Attorney's office interviewing an elderly female victim of an assault in order to prepare a list of charges.
   The one of the following which would be MOST important in determining all the facts is

   A. creating a close, cooperative working relationship with the victim
   B. establishing your authority at the beginning of the interview
   C. maintaining a relaxed atmosphere during the interview
   D. having access to the particular statutes which might apply to this case

7. A client is critical of the way he has been treated by government agencies in the past. A paralegal aide interviewing him defends the overall performance of government employees.
   This reaction by the aide is GENERALLY

   A. *appropriate;* the aide has an obligation to defend fellow workers in government service when such defense is justified
   B. *inappropriate;* the aide should remain neutral rather than volunteer his personal opinions
   C. *appropriate;* the aide should honestly express his personal opinions in such circumstances unless it is likely to provoke antagonism
   D. *inappropriate;* the aide should agree with the client's comments to help establish a greater rapport with him

Questions 8-11.

DIRECTIONS: Questions 8 through 11 are to be answered SOLELY on the basis of the following passage.

*A person may use physical force upon another person when and to the extent he reasonably believes such to be necessary to defend himself or a third person from what he reasonably believes to be the use or imminent use of unlawful physical force by such other person, unless (a) the latter's conduct was provoked by the actor himself with intent to cause physical injury to another person, or (b) the actor was the initial aggressor; or (c) the physical force involved is the product of a combat by agreement not specifically authorized by law.*

*A person may not use deadly physical force upon another person under the circumstances specified above unless: (a) he reasonably believes that such other person is using or is about to use deadly physical force. Even in such case, however, the actor may not use deadly physical force if he knows he can with complete safety as to himself and others avoid the necessity of doing so by retreating, except that he is under no duty to retreat if he is in his dwelling and is not the initial aggressor; or (b) he reasonably believes that such other person is committing or attempting to commit a kidnapping, forcible rape, or forcible sodomy.*

8. Jones and Smith, who have not met before, get into an argument in a tavern. Smith takes a punch at Jones but misses. Jones then hits Smith on the chin with his fist. Smith falls to the floor and suffers minor injuries. According to the above passage, it would be CORRECT to state that

    A. *only* Smith was justified in using physical force
    B. *only* Jones was justified in using physical force
    C. both Smith and Jones were justified in using physical force
    D. neither Smith nor Jones was justified in using physical force

9. While walking down the street, Brady observes Miller striking Mrs. Adams on the head with his fist in an attempt to steal her purse.
    According to the above passage, it would be CORRECT to state that Brady would

    A. not be justified in using deadly physical force against Miller since Brady can safety retreat
    B. be justified in using physical force against Miller, but not deadly physical force
    C. not be justified in using physical force against Miller since Brady himself is not being attacked
    D. be justified in using deadly physical force

10. Winters is attacked from behind by Sharp, who attempts to beat up Winters with a blackjack. Winters disarms Sharp and succeeds in subduing him with a series of blows to the head. Sharp stops fighting and explains that he thought Winters was the person who had robbed his apartment a few minutes before, but now realizes his mistake. According to the above passage, it would be CORRECT to state that

    A. Winters was justified in using physical force on Sharp only to the extent necessary to defend himself
    B. Winters was not justified in using physical force on Sharp since Sharp's attack was provoked by what he believed to be Winters' behavior
    C. Sharp was justified in using physical force on Winters since he reasonably believed that Winters had unlawfully robbed him
    D. Winters was justified in using physical force on Sharp only because Sharp was acting mistakenly in attacking him

11. Roberts hears a noise in the cellar of his home and, upon investigation, discovers an intruder, Welch. Welch moves towards Roberts in a threatening manner, thrusts his hand into a bulging pocket, and withdraws what appears to be a gun. Roberts thereupon strikes Welch over the head with a golf club. He then sees that the *gun* is a toy. Welch later dies of head injuries.
    According to the above passage, it would be CORRECT to state that Roberts

A. *was justified* in using deadly physical force because he reasonably believed Welch was about to use deadly physical force
B. *was not justified* in using deadly physical force
C. *was justified* in using deadly physical force only because he did not provoke Welch's conduct
D. *was justified* in using deadly physical force only because he was not the initial aggressor

Questions 12-15.

DIRECTIONS: Questions 12 through 15 are to be answered SOLELY on the basis of the following passage.

*From the beginning, the Supreme Court has supervised the fairness of trials conducted by the Federal government. But the Constitution, as originally drafted, gave the court no such general authority in state oases. The court's power to deal with state cases comes from the Fourteenth Amendment, which became part of the Constitution in 1868. The crucial provision forbids any state to "deprive any person of life, liberty or property without due process of law."*

*The guarantee of "due process" would seem, at the least, to require fair procedure in criminal trials. But curiously, the Supreme Court did not speak on the question for many decades. During that time, however, the due process clause was interpreted to bar "unreasonable" state economic regulations, such as minimum wage laws.*

*In 1915, there came the case of Leo M. Frank, a Georgian convicted of murder in a trial that he contended was dominated by mob hysteria. Historians now agree that there was such hysteria, with overtones of anti-semitism.*

*The Supreme Court held that it could not look past the findings of the Georgia courts that there had been no mob atmosphere at the trial. Justices Oliver Wendell Holmes and Charles Evans Hughes dissented, arguing that the constitutional guarantee would be "a barren one" if the Federal courts could not make their own inferences from the facts.*

*In 1923, the case of Moore v. Dempsey involved five Arkansas blacks convicted of murder and sentenced to death in a community so aroused against them that at one point they were saved from lynching only by Federal troops. Witnesses against them were said to have been beaten into testifying.*

*The court, though not actually setting aside the convictions, directed a lower Federal court to hold a habeas corpus hearing to find out whether the trial had been fair, or whether the whole proceeding had been "a mask — that counsel, jury, and judge were swept to the fatal end by an irresistible wave of public opinion."*

12. According to the above passage, the Supreme Court's INITIAL interpretation of the Fourteenth Amendment

    A. protected state supremacy in economic matters
    B. increased the scope of Federal jurisdiction
    C. required fair procedures in criminal trials
    D. prohibited the enactment of minimum wage laws

13. According to the above passage, the Supreme Court in the Frank case    13._____

    A. denied that there had been mob hysteria at the trial
    B. decided that the guilty verdict was supported by the evidence
    C. declined to question the state court's determination of the facts
    D. found that Leo Frank had not received *due process*

14. According to the above passage, the dissenting judges in the Frank case maintained that    14._____

    A. due process was an empty promise in the circumstances of that case
    B. the Federal courts could not guarantee certain provisions of the Constitution
    C. the Federal courts should not make their own inferences from the facts in state cases
    D. the Supreme Court had rendered the Constitution *barren*

15. Of the following, the MOST appropriate title for the above passage is:    15._____

    A. THE CONDUCT OF FEDERAL TRIALS
    B. THE DEVELOPMENT OF STATES' RIGHTS: 1868-1923
    C. MOORE V. DEMPSEY: A CASE STUDY IN CRIMINAL JUSTICE
    D. DUE PROCESS - THE EVOLUTION OF A CONSTITUTIONAL CORNERSTONE

# KEY (CORRECT ANSWERS)

1. B
2. D
3. C
4. A
5. C

6. A
7. B
8. B
9. B
10. A

11. A
12. D
13. C
14. A
15. D

# EXAMINATION SECTION
## TEST 1

DIRECTIONS: Each question or incomplete statement is followed by several suggested answers or completions. Select the one that BEST answers the question or completes the statement. *PRINT THE LETTER OF THE CORRECT ANSWER IN THE SPACE AT THE RIGHT.*

1. P and D signed a contract for the proposed sale of Blackacre. The contract included a description of the property, the selling price, the amount of the purchase money mortgage, and the identity of the parties. It further provided that terms for the payment of principal and interest would be mutually agreed upon at the time the formal contract was concluded. Subsequently, D prepared a contract which provided a schedule of amortization which P found unsatisfactory. P prepared another contract with a somewhat different schedule which he signed and forwarded to D.
D refused to sign and refused to go forward with the sale. P brings an action in specific performance.
In such a case, specific performance should be

   A. *denied* because a material element of the contract is left for future negotiations
   B. *denied* because the terms of the mortgage payments had been omitted; the absence of any element in a contract for the sale of real property vitiates the contract under the Statute of Frauds
   C. *granted* because the defendant cannot take advantage of the failure of a condition precedent where he himself has prevented the condition from being met
   D. *granted* because the contract meets the requirements of the Statute of Frauds, the buyer and seller, the property and the price all being identified

2. Which one of the following statements concerning consideration as an element in contracts is NOT accurate?

   A. Consideration may be defined as a bargained-for exchange.
   B. A promise to make a gift is unenforceable.
   C. An exclusive dealing agreement is not without consideration because the party who gets the exclusive right makes no promise in return; the law implies a duty to use his best efforts.
   D. An agreement which permits one of the parties to terminate at will is enforceable against the other party who did not retain such a right.

3. P entered into a written contract with D which provided that if P could obtain a dealership for D from X, P would receive $10,000 and a percentage of the profits.
P did obtain the dealership for D by bribing X's manager. D knew nothing of this. Subsequently, he does not pay P, and P brings an accounting action against D.
In such a case, P

   A. *can* recover because the contract is valid on its face and the illegal acts committed were not part of that agreement
   B. *cannot* recover because an agent may not recover from his principal compensation for obtaining a contract by illegal means not authorized by the principal
   C. *can* recover because D cannot assert as a defense a wrong committed against X
   D. *cannot* recover because of his illegal conduct but D cannot benefit thereby; D must hold the profits and the $10,000 as a constructive trustee for the benefit of X

4. P, who had a government contract for radar sets, entered into a contract with D for gears needed to construct the sets. Subsequently, P obtained an additional contract for such sets from the Government and advertised for bids for the gears he would need for the second contract. D notified P that unless he gave him the contract for the additional gears and agreed to pay him a higher price on all gears furnished, including the ones needed for the first contract, he would refuse to supply him with any gears at all. Because of the liquidated damage and default clauses in P's contract with the Government and his inability to get enough gears to meet his commitments on the first contract if D breached, P agreed to D's demands and entered into a new contract for all the gears at a higher price. Subsequently, P sued D to recover payments made for goods delivered
In such a case, P

4.____

    A. *should succeed* because the contract was voidable on the grounds of duress
    B. *should lose* because, although he was subject to economic duress, the duress that avoids a contract is physical duress or fear of physical duress
    C. *should lose* because there was a recission of the first contract and a valid new contract
    D. *should succeed* partially because there was no consideration for the new price charged for the gears; P should recover the difference between the old contract price and the new contract price for the gears furnished for the first contract

5. Which one of the following is NOT a proper rule of damages for breach of a contract of sale of merchandise to be resold by a purchaser?

5.____

    A. The general rule is that the buyer who has contracted to resell goods to a customer is entitled to the difference between the market price on the date of the breach and the price he must pay for cover. In anticipatory breach, he may select either the contract date or the date he was notified that the seller would not perform.
    B. If there are special circumstances made known to the seller at the time the contract was made that put him on notice that his failure to deliver would cause the buyer to breach a contract with his customer, and in fact that second contract is breached, the measure of damages is the damages paid by the buyer to his customer and expenses incurred to satisfy the buyer's breach to this customer.
    C. If the breach is not substantial, the measure of damages is the difference between the value of full performance and the value of the performance that was proffered, or the cost of replacing the non-conforming goods, whichever is more; no buyer has a right to reject goods which substantially conform to the contract.
    D. Mere knowledge by seller that buyer is purchasing for resale is not deemed notice of special circumstances that would entitle the buyer to recover consequential damages.

6. When researching a legal problem, the main objective is to locate primary (mandatory) authority within your jurisdiction.
Primary authority would NOT include

6.____

    A. legislation
    B. judicial decisions
    C. administrative rules
    D. law revision commission reports

7. Assume that you are given the name of a case and the citation to either the official reports or unofficial reporter in which it is published.
   The one of the following you should consult in order to obtain the parallel citation is

   A. the state Jurisprudence
   B. Shepard Case Citators
   C. the state Consolidated Laws Service
   D. Corpus Juris Secundum

8. Absent primary (mandatory) authority within this state relating to a legal question under consideration, you would consider persuasive (secondary) authority. Persuasive authority would NOT include

   A. other-state judicial decisions
   B. opinions of legal experts
   C. legislation of another state
   D. obiter dictum in reporter opinions

9. Where there has been no judicial interpretation relevant to a particular legal issue, what source other than the statute itself would you consult in order to determine the existence of documentation which might indicate the legislative intent of a statute enacted by the legislature of the state?

   A. American Jurisprudence 2nd
   B. Manual for the use of the Legislature of the State
   C. McKinney's Session Laws
   D. Abbott's Digest

10. Shepard Case Citators enable you to determine whether the cited case

    A. has been affirmed, reversed, or modified on appeal to a higher tribunal
    B. has been subsequently modified by a statute
    C. is discussed in Corpus Juris Secundum
    D. is listed in the Annotations in McKinney's Consolidated Laws

11. The Shepard Citator unit for Statutes does NOT permit you to shepardize

    A. opinions of the Attorney General of the United States
    B. United States Code
    C. United States treaties
    D. Unconsolidated Laws (McKinney)

12. Assume that you commence your research by using Abbott's Digest and find no cases under the Topic and Key Number assigned to your point of law.
    In this situation, by using the same Topic and Key Number, you can extend your search to all of the following EXCEPT

    A. the Atlantic Digest
    B. the American Digest System
    C. Modern Federal Practice Digest
    D. American Law Reports 2d Digest

13. Rules promulgated by the Courts of the State are published in all of the following publications EXCEPT

    A. State Official Compilation of Codes, Rules, and Regulations
    B. Abbott's Digest
    C. New York Law Journal
    D. McKinney's Consolidated Laws

14. Which of the following is the official report in which cases decided by the New York Court of Appeals are published?

    A. Northeastern Reporter 2d
    B. New York Supplement 2d
    C. New York Reports 2d
    D. Miscellaneous Reports 2d

15. In tracing federal legislative history, all of the following should be considered in order to assist in determining the intent of Congress EXCEPT

    A. Congressional debates
    B. U.S. Government Manual, 1973-1974
    C. Congressional Committee published reports
    D. Congressional Committee published hearings

16. According to the Uniform System of Citations, 11th ed., which one of the following examples would be the proper method of citing the case of Courtney v. Kelmus, decided in the Supreme Court, State of New York, on December 1, 1944, and reported in volume 50 of the New York Supplement 2d on page 897 and in volume 182 of the Miscellaneous Reports on page 498?

    A. 182 Misc. 498, 50 N.Y.S.2d 897
    B. 50 N.Y.S.2d 897, 182 Misc. 498 (Sup. Ct. 1944)
    C. 182 Misc. 498 (Sup. Ct. 1944)
    D. 182 Misc. 498, 50 N.Y.S.2d 897 (Sup. Ct. 1944)

Questions 17-25.

DIRECTIONS: Questions 17 through 25 are to be answered SOLELY on the basis of case law and statutory law in the State.

17. What jurisdiction does the State acquire when a foreign corporation is *doing business* in this state?
    The State

    A. acquires personal jurisdiction over the foreign corporation for any cause of action, no matter where the events which gave rise to it occurred
    B. acquires jurisdiction over only those acts committed by the foreign corporation in the State
    C. always acquires jurisdiction over all of the foreign corporation's foreign subsidiaries
    D. acquires no jurisdiction unless the foreign corporation's property can be attached

18. A defendant does NOT appear in an action when he

    A. makes a motion which has the effect of extending the time to answer
    B. serves a timely answer
    C. demands a complaint if one is not served with the summons in an action of the Supreme Court
    D. serves a timely notice of appearance

19. With respect to the granting of an order of attachment, it would be CORRECT to state that such an order

    A. may be granted in a matrimonial action
    B. must be granted where defendant is not a resident or domiciliary of the state and plaintiff would be entitled to a money judgment
    C. is never granted against a New York domiciliary
    D. may be granted where defendant is not a resident or domiciliary of the state and plaintiff would be entitled to a money judgment

20. Which of the following is NOT the function of a bill of particulars?
    To

    A. amplify the pleadings
    B. obtain your adversary's evidence
    C. limit proof at trial
    D. prevent surprise at trial

21. Which of the following statements concerning a motion for summary judgement is NOT correct?

    A. Without a formal cross-motion, the court cannot grant summary judgment to a non-moving party.
    B. The motion shall be granted if the cause of action is established sufficiently to warrant the court as a matter of law in directing judgment.
    C. The motion shall be denied if there is a genuine factual issue requiring a trial.
    D. An affidavit by an attorney without personal knowledge of the facts is of no probative value.

22. Plaintiff may NOT conduct an examination before trial

    A. of a third-party defendant
    B. of a defendant unless plaintiff first obtains a court order
    C. of a non-party witness unless there are special circumstances shown
    D. unless a note of issue and statement of readiness have been filed

23. In a medical malpractice action based on defendant's alleged negligence in leaving a surgical clamp inside plaintiff, the statute of limitations

    A. begins to run from the date of the operation
    B. may be extended by the court upon a showing of good cause
    C. need not be pleaded as an affirmative defense
    D. will not begin to run until plaintiff could reasonably have discovered the malpractice

24. When jurisdiction is acquired over a defendant solely on the basis of the *Long-arm* statute (CPLR 302), it would be CORRECT to state that

    A. New York has jurisdiction over every tortious act committed by the defendant outside New York causing injury to property within New York
    B. New York has jurisdiction over a cause of action against a New Jersey domiciliary who drives into New York and runs over plaintiff
    C. defendant's appearance in New York gives the court jurisdiction over causes of action not arising from acts enumerated in the statute
    D. defendant's ownership of real property in New York gives the court jurisdiction over every tortious act committed by him outside New York

25. Where plaintiff joins a claim that is not triable by jury with a claim that is triable by jury as of right, the plaintiff

    A. is entitled to a trial by jury on both claims of action
    B. has split his cause of action
    C. has waived his right to a jury trial on both claims where the claims are based on the same transactions and wrongs
    D. is entitled to a trial by jury only on the claim triable by jury as of right

## KEY (CORRECT ANSWERS)

| | | | |
|---|---|---|---|
| 1. A | | 11. A | |
| 2. D | | 12. D | |
| 3. B | | 13. B | |
| 4. A | | 14. C | |
| 5. C | | 15. D | |
| 6. D | | 16. D | |
| 7. B | | 17. A | |
| 8. C | | 18. C | |
| 9. C | | 19. D | |
| 10. A | | 20. B | |

21. A
22. C
23. D
24. B
25. C

# INTERVIEWING
# EXAMINATION SECTION
# TEST 1

DIRECTIONS: Each question or incomplete statement is followed by several suggested answers or completions. Select the one that BEST answers the question or completes the statement. *PRINT THE LETTER OF THE CORRECT ANSWER IN THE SPACE AT THE RIGHT.*

1. Of the following, the BEST way for an interviewer to calm a person who seems to have become emotionally upset as a result of a question asked is for the interviewer to

   A. talk to the person about other things for a short time
   B. ask that the person control himself
   C. probe for the cause of his emotional upset
   D. finish the questioning as quickly as possible

   1.____

2. You find that an applicant is hesitant about showing you some required personal material and documents. Your *initial* reaction to this situation should be to

   A. quietly insist that he give you the required materials
   B. make an exception in his case to avoid making him uncomfortable
   C. suspect that he may be trying to withhold evidence
   D. understand that he is in a stressful situation and may feel ashamed to reveal such information

   2.____

3. An applicant has just given you a response which does not seem clear.
   Of the following, the BEST course of action for you to take in order to check your understanding of the applicant's response is for you to

   A. ask the question again during a subsequent interview with this applicant
   B. repeat the applicant's answer in the applicant's own words and ask if that is what the applicant meant
   C. later in the interview, repeat the question that led to this response
   D. repeat the question that led to this response, but say it more forcefully

   3.____

4. While speaking with applicants, you may find that there are times when an applicant will be silent for a short while before answering questions.
   In order to gather the best information from the applicant, the interviewer should *generally* treat these silences by

   A. repeating the same question to make the applicant stop hesitating
   B. rephrasing the question in a way that the applicant can answer it faster
   C. directing an easier question to the applicant so that he can gain confidence in answering
   D. waiting patiently and not pressuring the applicant into quick, undeveloped answers

   4.____

5. In dealing with members of *different* ethnic and religious groups among the applicants you interview, you should give

   A. individuals the services to which they are entitled
   B. less service to those you judge to be more advantaged

   5.____

C. better service to groups with which you sympathize most
D. better service to groups with political "muscle"

6. You must be sure that, when interviewing an applicant, you phrase each question carefully.
   Of the following, the MOST important reason for this is to insure that

   A. the applicant will phrase each of his responses carefully
   B. you use correct grammar
   C. it is clear to the applicant what information you are seeking
   D. you do not word the same question differently for different applicants

7. When given a form to complete, a client hesitates, tells you that he cannot fill out forms too well and that he is afraid he will do a poor job. He asks you to do it for him. You are quite sure, however, that he is able to do it himself.
   In this case, it would be MOST advisable for you to

   A. encourage him to try filling out the application as well as he can
   B. fill out the application for him
   C. explain to him that he must learn to accept responsibility
   D. tell him that, if others can fill out an application, he can too

8. Assume that an applicant whom you are interviewing has made a statement that is obviously not true.
   Of the following, the BEST course of action for you to take at this point in the interview is to

   A. ask the applicant if he is sure about his statement
   B. tell the applicant that his statement is incorrect
   C. question the applicant further to clarify his response
   D. assume that the statement is correct

9. Assume that you are conducting an *initial* interview with an applicant.
   Of the following, the MOST advisable questions for you to ask at the beginning of this interview are those that

   A. can be answered in one or two sentences
   B. have nothing to do with the subject matter of the interview
   C. are most likely to reveal any hostility on the part of the applicant
   D. the applicant is most likely to be willing and able to answer

10. When interviewing a particularly nervous and upset applicant, the one of the following actions which you should take FIRST is to

    A. inform the applicant that, to be helped, he must cooperate
    B. advise the applicant that proof must be provided for statements he makes
    C. assure the applicant that every effort will be made to provide him with whatever assistance he is entitled to
    D. tell the applicant he will have no trouble so long as he is truthful

11. Assume that it is part of your job to prepare a monthly report for your unit head that eventually goes to the director. The report contains information on the number of applicants you have interviewed that have been approved and the number of applicants you have interviewed that have been turned down. Errors on such reports are *serious* because

    A. you are expected to be able to prove how many applicants you have interviewed each month
    B. accurate statistics are needed for effective management of the department
    C. they may not be discovered before the report is transmitted to the director
    D. they may result in a loss to the applicants left out of the report

12. During interviews, people give information about themselves in several ways.
    Which of the following *usually* gives the LEAST amount of information about the person being questioned? His

    A. spoken words
    B. tone of voice
    C. facial expression
    D. body position

13. Suppose an applicant, while being interviewed, becomes angered by your questioning and begins to use sharp, uncontrolled language.
    Which of the following is the BEST way for you to react to him?

    A. Speak in his style to show him that you are neither impressed nor upset by his speech
    B. Interrupt him and tell him that you are not required to listen to this kind of speech
    C. Lower your voice and slow the rate of your speech in an attempt to set an example that will calm him
    D. Let him continue in his way but insist that he answer your questions directly

14. You have been informed that no determination has yet been made on the eligibility of an applicant whom you have interviewed. The decision depends on further checking. His situation, however, is similar to that of many other applicants whose eligibility has been approved. The applicant, *quite worried,* calls you, and asks whether his application has been accepted.
    What would be BEST for you to do under these circumstances? Tell him

    A. his application is being checked and you will let him know the final result as soon as possible
    B. that a written request addressed to your supervisor will probably get faster action for his case
    C. not to worry since other applicants with similar backgrounds have already been accepted
    D. since there is no definite information and you are very busy, you will call him back

15. Suppose that you have been talking with an applicant. You have the feeling from the latest things the applicant has said that some of his answers to earlier questions were not totally correct. You guess that he might have been afraid or confused earlier but that your conversation has now put him in a more comfortable frame of mind.
    In order to test the reliability of information received from the earlier questions, the BEST thing for you to do *now* is to ask new questions that

A. allow the applicant to explain why he deliberately gave false information to you
B. ask for the same information, although worded differently from the original questions
C. put pressure on the applicant so that he personally wants to clear up the facts in his earlier answers
D. indicate to the applicant that you are aware of his deceptiveness

16. While providing you with required information, an applicant whom you are interviewing, informs you that she does not know certain facts.
Of the following, the MOST advisable action for you to take is to

    A. ask her to explain further
    B. advise her about research facilities
    C. express your sympathy for the situation
    D. go on to the next item of information

16.____

17. If, in an interview, you wish to determine a client's usual occupation, which one of the following questions is MOST likely to elicit the *most* useful information?

    A. Did you ever work in a factory?
    B. Do you know how to do office work?
    C. What kind of work do you do?
    D. Where are you working now?

17.____

18. Assume that you are approached by a clerk from another office who starts questioning you about one of the clients you have just interviewed. The clerk says that she is a relative of the client. According to departmental policy, all matters discussed with clients are to be kept confidential.
Of the following, the BEST course of action for you to take in this situation would be to

    A. check to see whether the clerk is really a relative before you make any further decisions
    B. explain to the clerk why you cannot divulge the information
    C. tell the clerk that you do not know the answers to her questions
    D. tell the clerk that she can get from the client any information the client wishes to give

18.____

19. Which of the following is usually the BEST technique for you, as an interviewer, to use to bring an applicant back to subject matter from which the applicant has strayed?

    A. Ask the applicant a question that is related to the subject of the interview
    B. Show the applicant that his response is unrelated to the question
    C. Discreetly reind the applicant that there is a time allotment for the interview
    D. Tell the applicant that you will be happy to discuss the extraneous matters at a future interview

19.____

20. Assume that you are interviewing a witness who is telling a story crucial to your investigation. It is important that you get all the facts being related by this witness. In order to secure this vital information, the BEST of the following techniques is to

    A. quietly interrupt the witness's story and request him to speak with deliberation so that you can record his statement
    B. guide the witness during his recital so that all important points are validated

20.____

C. confine your activities during the story to brief note-taking, and, after the information has been secured, request a full written statement
D. inform the witness that he must relate all the facts as truthfully and concisely as possible

21. The statement of any witness obtained in an interview should GENERALLY be considered

    A. as a lead requiring substantiation by additional evidence
    B. accurate if the witness appears honest and is cooperative
    C. unreliable if the witness has been involved in similar investigations
    D. as a fact admissible under the rules of evidence

22. During an important interview, an interviewer takes notes from time to time but very rarely looks at the subject being questioned.
Such action on the part of the interviewer is

    A. *unacceptable,* chiefly because during the actual interview an interviewer should pay more attention to the witness's manner of giving the information rather than to the content of his statements
    B. *acceptable,* chiefly because data should be recorded at the earliest opportunity and important data should be noted meticulously
    C. *unacceptable,* chiefly because it inhibits the person being interviewed and is not conducive to a give-and-take discussion
    D. *unacceptable,* chiefly because focusing attention on note-taking and not on the person being interviewed creates an impression of professional objectivity

23. Since he must interview persons with various personalities and attitudes, an interviewer should, *generally,* adopt a method of interviewing that

    A. is uniformly applicable to all types so that discrepancies in the accounts of individuals may be readily detected
    B. can be adjusted to the persons whom he interviews
    C. is based on the premise that most interviewees tend to be uncooperative
    D. requires the interviewer to spend as little time as possible in questioning applicants

24. One of the more difficult tasks facing an interviewer is to control the tendency of witnesses to ramble when giving information.
Of the following, the BEST technique for keeping a witness's comments pertinent is to

    A. ask questions which indicate the desired answer
    B. insist on "yes" and "no" answers to his questions
    C. construct questions that restrict the range of information which the witness can give in response
    D. ask precise questions so that the answers of the witness will necessarily be brief

25. During interviews, a certain interviewer phrases follow-up questions mentally during pauses while the subject is still answering the previous question. This practice is, *generally,*
    A. *desirable,* chiefly because it gives the impression that the interviewer is well acquainted with all the facts
    B. *undesirable,* chiefly because the interviewer cannot know whether such questions will be appropriate
    C. *desirable,* chiefly because it enables the interviewer to pose new questions without significant breaks in the discussion
    D. *undesirable,* chiefly because it subjects the person being interviewed to a barrage of questions

25.____

## KEY (CORRECT ANSWERS)

1. A
2. D
3. B
4. D
5. A

6. C
7. A
8. C
9. D
10. C

11. B
12. D
13. C
14. A
15. B

16. D
17. C
18. B
19. A
20. C

21. A
22. C
23. B
24. C
25. C

# TEST 2

DIRECTIONS: Each question or incomplete statement is followed by several suggested answers or completions. Select the one that BEST answers the question or completes the statement. *PRINT THE LETTER OF THE CORRECT ANSWER IN THE SPACE AT THE RIGHT.*

1. The one of the following which is the BEST description of a *properly* objective interviewer is one who

    A. is friendly and sensitive to the client's feelings, without becoming emotionally involved
    B. is distant and impersonal, remaining unaffected by what the client says
    C. lets personal emotions enter as far as the client's situation calls for them
    D. becomes emotionally involved with the client's situation, but without showing this involvement

    1.____

2. The one of the following which is MOST necessary for successfully intefviewing a person who belongs to a culture different from that of the interviewer is for the interviewer to

    A. have some appreciation of the other culture
    B. ignore those cultural differences which lead to bias
    C. stay away from sensitive, "touchy" issues
    D. assume the mannerisms of people in the other culture

    2.____

3. In fact-finding interviews, it is generally assumed that the smaller the lumber of interviewees, the greater the increase of reliability with the addition of others.
   The PROPER number of interviewees needed to insure the accuracy of information obtained *generally* depends upon the

    A. educational level of those interviewed
    B. number of people who have the required information
    C. directness of the questions asked
    D. variability of the information received

    3.____

4. The one of the following which is generally MOST likely to be *accurately* described in an interview by an interviewee is

    A. the presence of a large painting in the interviewer's office
    B. the number of people in the interviewer's waiting room
    C. space relations
    D. duration of time

    4.____

5. The one of the following which is *generally* the BEST course of action for an interviewer to take when interviewing a person who is reluctant to tell what he knows about a matter under investigation is to

    A. be curt and abrupt, and threaten the person with the consequences of his withholding information
    B. be firm and severe, and pressure the person into telling the needed information

    5.____

C. be patient and candid with the person being questioned about the investigation since doing otherwise is not ethical
D. give the person false information about the investigation so he will give the needed information without realizing its importance

6. It is often recommended that an interviewer prepare in advance a list of questions or topics to be covered in an interview.
The MAIN reason for using such a checklist is to

   A. allow investigations to be assigned to less efficient interviewers
   B. eliminate a large amount of follow-up paper work
   C. aid the interviewer in remembering to cover all important topics
   D. aid the interviewer in maintaining an objective distance from the person interviewed

7. *Usually,* the CHIEF advantage of a directive approach in an interview is that the

   A. interviewer maintains control over the course of the interview
   B. person interviewed is more likely to be put at ease
   C. person interviewed is generally left free to direct the interview
   D. interviewer will not suggest answers to the person interviewed

8. *Usually,* the CHIEF advantage of a non-directive approach in conducting an interview is that the

   A. interviewer generally conceals what he is looking for in the interview
   B. person interviewed is more likely to express his true feelings about the topic under discussion
   C. person interviewed is more likely to follow an idea introduced by the interviewer
   D. interviewer can keep the discussion limited to topics he believes to be relevant

9. The one of the following which is generally the LEAST likely to be *accurate* in a description of an event given to an interviewer is a statement about

   A. the presence of an object
   B. the number of people, when their number is small
   C. locations of people
   D. duration of time

10. Assume that you, an interviewer, are conducting a character investigation.
In an interview, the one of the following character traits of the person being interviewed which can *usually* be determined with a GOOD degree of reliability is

    A. honesty            B. dependability
    C. forcefulness       D. perseverance

11. You have been assigned the task of obtaining a family's social history.
The BEST place for you to interview members of the family while obtaining this social history would, *generally,* be in

    A. the family's home
    B. your agency's general offices
    C. the home of a friend of the family
    D. your own private office

12. If an interviewer obtains testimony from persons in interviews by means of interrogation or asking questions rather than by letting the person freely relate the testimony, what is said will, *generally,* be

    A. *greater* in range and *less* accurate
    B. *greater* in range and *more* accurate
    C. about the *same* in range and *less* accurate
    D. about the *same* in range and *more* accurate

12.____

13. Experienced interviewers have learned to phrase their questions carefully in order to obtain the desired response. Of the following, the question which would *usually* elicit the MOST accurate answer is:

    A. "How old are you?"
    B. "What is your income?"
    C. "How are you today?"
    D. "What is your date of birth?"

13.____

14. The one of the following questions which would *generally* lead to the LEAST reliable answer is:

    A. "Did you see a wallet?"
    B. "Was the German Shepherd gray?"
    C. "Didn't you see the stop sign?"
    D. "Did you see the guard on duty?"

14.____

15. Some interviewers may make a practice of observing details of the surroundings when interviewing in someone's home or office.
    Such a practice is, *generally,* considered

    A. *undesirable,* mainly because such snooping is an unwarranted, unethical invasion of privacy
    B. *undesirable,* mainly because useful information is rarely, if ever, gained this way
    C. *desirable,* mainly because useful insights into the character of the person interviewed may be gained
    D. *desirable,* mainly because it is impossible to evaluate a person adequately without such observation of his environment

15.____

## KEY (CORRECT ANSWERS)

| | | | | | |
|---|---|---|---|---|---|
| 1. | A | 6. | C | 11. | A |
| 2. | A | 7. | A | 12. | A |
| 3. | D | 8. | B | 13. | D |
| 4. | A | 9. | D | 14. | B |
| 5. | C | 10. | C | 15. | C |

# EXAMINATION SECTION
# TEST 1

DIRECTIONS: Each question or incomplete statement is followed by several suggested answers or completions. Select the one that BEST answers the question or completes the statement. *PRINT THE LETTER OF THE CORRECT ANSWER IN THE SPACE AT THE RIGHT.*

Questions 1-9.

DIRECTIONS: Questions 1 through 9 consist of sentences which may or may not be examples of good English usage. Consider grammar, punctuation, spelling, capitalization, awkwardness, etc. Examine each sentence, and then choose the correct statement about it from the four choices below it. If the English usage in the sentence given is better than it would be with any of the changes suggested in options B, C, and D, choose option A. Do not choose an option that will change the meaning of the sentence.

1. According to Judge Frank, the grocer's sons found guilty of assault and sentenced last Thursday.

    A. This is an example of acceptable writing.
    B. A comma should be placed after the word *sentenced*.
    C. The word *were* should be placed after *sons*
    D. The apostrophe in *grocer's* should be placed after the *s*.

    1.____

2. The department heads assistant said that the stenographers should type duplicate copies of all contracts, leases, and bills.

    A. This is an example of acceptable writing.
    B. A comma should be placed before the word *contracts.*
    C. An apostrophe should be placed before the *s* in *heads*.
    D. Quotation marks should be placed before *the stenographers* and after *bills*.

    2.____

3. The lawyers questioned the men to determine who was the true property owner?

    A. This is an example of acceptable writing.
    B. The phrase *questioned the men* should be changed to *asked the men questions*.
    C. The word *was* should be changed to *were*.
    D. The question mark should be changed to a period.

    3.____

4. The terms stated in the present contract are more specific than those stated in the previous contract.

    A. This is an example of acceptable writing.
    B. The word *are* should be changed to *is*.
    C. The word *than* should be changed to *then*.
    D. The word *specific* should be changed to *specified*.

    4.____

5. Of the lawyers considered, the one who argued more skillful was chosen for the job.

    A. This is an example of acceptable writing.
    B. The word *more* should be replaced by the word *most*.
    C. The word *skillful* should be replaced by the word *skillfully,*
    D. The word *chosen* should be replaced by the word *selected*.

    5.____

6. Each of the states has a court of appeals; some states have circuit courts. 6._____

   A. This is an example of acceptable writing.
   B. The semi-colon should be changed to a comma.
   C. The word *has* should be changed to *have*.
   D. The word *some* should be capitalized.

7. The court trial has greatly effected the child's mental condition. 7._____

   A. This is an example of acceptable writing.
   B. The word *effected* should be changed to *affected*.
   C. The word *greatly* should be placed after *effected*.
   D. The apostrophe in *child's* should be placed after the *s*.

8. Last week, the petition signed by all the officers was sent to the Better Business Bureau. 8._____

   A. This is an example of acceptable writing.
   B. The phrase *last week* should be placed after *officers*.
   C. A comma should be placed after *petition*.
   D. The word *was* should be changed to *were*.

9. Mr. Farrell claims that he requested form A-12, and three booklets describing court procedures. 9._____

   A. This is an example of acceptable writing.
   B. The word *that* should be eliminated.
   C. A colon should be placed after *requested*.
   D. The comma after *A-12* should be eliminated.

Questions 10-21.

DIRECTIONS: Questions 10 through 21 contain a word in capital letters followed by four suggested meanings of the word. For each question, choose the BEST meaning for the word in capital letters.

10. SIGNATORY - A 10._____

    A. lawyer who draws up a legal document
    B. document that must be signed by a judge
    C. person who signs a document
    D. true copy of a signature

11. RETAINER - A 11._____

    A. fee paid to a lawyer for his services
    B. document held by a third party
    C. court decision to send a prisoner back to custody pending trial
    D. legal requirement to keep certain types of files

12. BEQUEATH - To 12._____

    A. receive assistance from a charitable organization
    B. give personal property by will to another
    C. transfer real property from one person to another
    D. receive an inheritance upon the death of a relative

13. RATIFY - To

    A. approve and sanction
    B. forego
    C. produce evidence
    D. summarize

14. CODICIL - A

    A. document introduced in evidence in a civil action
    B. subsection of a law
    C. type of legal action that can be brought by a plaintiff
    D. supplement or an addition to a will

15. ALIAS

    A. Assumed name
    B. In favor of
    C. Against
    D. A writ

16. PROXY - A(n)

    A. phony document in a real estate transaction
    B. opinion by a judge of a civil court
    C. document containing appointment of an agent
    D. summons in a lawsuit

17. ALLEGED

    A. Innocent
    B. Asserted
    C. Guilty
    D. Called upon

18. EXECUTE - To

    A. complete a legal document by signing it
    B. set requirements
    C. render services to a duly elected executive of a municipality
    D. initiate legal action such as a lawsuit

19. NOTARY PUBLIC - A

    A. lawyer who is running for public office
    B. judge who hears minor cases
    C. public officer, one of whose functions is to administer oaths
    D. lawyer who gives free legal services to persons unable to pay

20. WAIVE - To

    A. disturb a calm state of affairs
    B. knowingly renounce a right or claim
    C. pardon someone for a minor fault
    D. purposely mislead a person during an investigation

21. ARRAIGN - To

    A. prevent an escape
    B. defend a prisoner
    C. verify a document
    D. accuse in a court of law

Questions 22-40.

DIRECTIONS: Questions 22 through 40 each consist of four words which may or may not be spelled correctly. If you find an error in
only one word, mark your answer A;
any two words, mark your answer B;
any three words, mark your answer C;
none of these words, mark your answer D.

| | | | | | |
|---|---|---|---|---|---|
| 22. | occurrence | Febuary | privilege | similiar | 22.____ |
| 23. | separate | transferring | analyze | column | 23.____ |
| 24. | develop | license | bankrupcy | abreviate | 24.____ |
| 25. | subpoena | arguement | dissolution | foreclosure | 25.____ |
| 26. | exaggerate | fundamental | significance | warrant | 26.____ |
| 27. | citizen | endorsed | marraige | appraissal | 27.____ |
| 28. | precedant | univercity | observence | preliminary | 28.____ |
| 29. | stipulate | negligence | judgment | prominent | 29.____ |
| 30. | judisial | whereas | release | guardian | 30.____ |
| 31. | appeal | larcenny | transcrip | jurist | 31.____ |
| 32. | petition | tenancy | agenda | insurance | 32.____ |
| 33. | superfical | premise | morgaged | maintainance | 33.____ |
| 34. | testamony | publically | installment | possessed | 34.____ |
| 35. | escrow | decree | eviction | miscelaneous | 35.____ |
| 36. | securitys | abeyance | adhere | corporate | 36.____ |
| 37. | kaleidoscope | anesthesia | vermilion | tafetta | 37.____ |
| 38. | congruant | barrenness | plebescite | vigilance | 38.____ |
| 39. | picnicing | promisory | resevoir | omission | 39.____ |
| 40. | supersede | banister | wholly | seize | 40.____ |

## KEY (CORRECT ANSWERS)

| | | | | | | | |
|---|---|---|---|---|---|---|---|
| 1. | C | 11. | A | 21. | D | 31. | B |
| 2. | C | 12. | B | 22. | B | 32. | D |
| 3. | D | 13. | A | 23. | D | 33. | C |
| 4. | A | 14. | D | 24. | B | 34. | B |
| 5. | C | 15. | A | 25. | A | 35. | A |
| 6. | A | 16. | C | 26. | D | 36. | A |
| 7. | B | 17. | B | 27. | B | 37. | A |
| 8. | A | 18. | A | 28. | C | 38. | B |
| 9. | D | 19. | C | 29. | D | 39. | C |
| 10. | C | 20. | B | 30. | A | 40. | D |

# EXAMINATION SECTION
## TEST 1

DIRECTIONS: Each question or incomplete statement is followed by several suggested answers or completions. Select the one that BEST answers the question or completes the statement. *PRINT THE LETTER OF THE CORRECT ANSWER IN THE SPACE AT THE RIGHT.*

Questions 1-6.

DIRECTIONS: Questions 1 through 6 consist of descriptions of material to which a filing designation must be assigned.

Assume that the matters and cases described in the questions were referred for handling to a government legal office which has its files set up according to these file designations. The file designation consists of a number of characters and punctuation marks as described below.

The first character refers to agencies whose legal work is handled by this office. These agencies are numbered consecutively in the order in which they first submit a matter for attention, and are identified in an alphabetical card index. To date numbers have been assigned to agencies as follows:

| | |
|---|---|
| Department of Correction | 1 |
| Police Department | 2 |
| Department of Traffic | 3 |
| Department of Consumer Affairs | 4 |
| Commission on Human Rights | 5 |
| Board of Elections | 6 |
| Department of Personnel | 7 |
| Board of Estimate | 8 |

The second character is separated from the first character by a dash. The second character is the last digit of the year in which a particular lawsuit or matter is referred to the legal office.

The third character is separated from the second character by a colon and may consist of either of the following:

I. A sub-number assigned to each lawsuit to which the agency is a party. Lawsuits are numbered consecutively regardless of year. (Lawsuits are brought by or against agency heads rather than agencies themselves, but references are made to agencies for the purpose of simplification.)

or II. A capital letter assigned to each matter other than a lawsuit according to subject, the subject being identified in an alphabetical index. To date, letters have been assigned to subjects as follows:

| | | | | |
|---|---|---|---|---|
| Citizenship | A | | Housing | E |
| Discrimination | B | | Gambling | F |
| Residence Requirements | C | | Freedom of Religion | G |
| Civil Service Examinations | D | | | |

2 (#1)

*These referrals are numbered consecutively regardless of year. The first referral by a particular agency on citizenship, for example, would be designated A1, followed by A2, A3, etc.*

*If no reference is made in a question as to how many letters involving a certain subject or how many lawsuits have been referred by an agency, assume that it is the first.*

*For each question, choose the file designation which is MOST appropriate for filing the material described in the question.*

1. In January 2010, two candidates in a 2009 civil service examination for positions with the Department of Correction filed a suit against the Department of Personnel seeking to set aside an educational requirement for the title.
   The Department of Personnel immediately referred the lawsuit to the legal office for handling.

   A.  1-9:1        B.  1-0:D1        C.  7-9:D1        D.  7-0:1

2. In 2014, the Police Department made its sixth request for an opinion on whether an employee assignment proposed for 2015 could be considered discriminatory.

   A.  2-5:1-B6     B.  2-4:6         C.  2-4:1-B6      D.  2-4:B6

3. In 2015, a lawsuit was brought by the Bay Island Action Committee against the Board of Estimate in which the plaintiff sought withdrawal of approval of housing for the elderly in the Bay Island area given by the Board in 2015.

   A.  8-3:1        B.  8-5:1         C.  8-3:B1        D.  8-5:E1

4. In December 2014, community leaders asked the Police Department to ban outdoor meetings of a religious group on the grounds that the meetings were disrupting the area. Such meetings had been held from time to time during 2014. On January 31, 2015, the Police Department asked the government legal office for an opinion on whether granting this request would violate the worshippers' right to freedom of religion.

   A.  2-4:G-1      B.  2-5:G1        C.  2-5:B-1       D.  2-4:B1

5. In 2014, a woman filed suit against the Board of Elections. She alleged that she had not been permitted to vote at her usual polling place in the 2013 election and had been told she was not registered there. She claimed that she had always voted there and that her record card had been lost. This was the fourth case of its type for this agency.

   A.  6-4:4        B.  6-3:C4        C.  3-4:6         D.  6-3:4

6. A lawsuit was brought in 2011 by the Ace Pinball Machine Company against the Commissioner of Consumer Affairs. The lawsuit contested an ordinance which banned the use of pinball machines on the ground that they are gambling devices.
   This was the third lawsuit to which the Department of Consumer Affairs was a party.

   A.  4-1:1        B.  4-3:F1        C.  4-1:3         D.  3F-4:1

7. You are instructed by your supervisor to type a statement that must be signed by the person making the statement and by three witnesses to the signature. The typed statement will take two pages and will leave no room for signatures if the normal margin is maintained at the bottom of the second page.
   In this situation, the PREFERRED method is to type

   A. the signature lines below the normal margin on the second page
   B. nothing further and have the witnesses sign without a typed signature line
   C. the signature lines on a third page
   D. some of the text and the signature lines on a third page

8. Certain legal documents always begin with a statement of venue - that is, the county and state in which the document is executed. This is usually boxed with a parentheses or colons.
   The one of the following documents that ALWAYS bears a statement of venue in a prominent position at its head is a(n)

   A. affidavit            B. memorandum of law
   C. contract of sale     D. will

9. A court stenographer is to take stenographic notes and transcribe the statements of a person under oath. The person has a heavy accent and speaks in ungrammatical and broken English.
   When he or she is transcribing the testimony, of the following, the BEST thing for them to do is to

   A. transcribe the testimony exactly as spoken, making no grammatical changes
   B. make only the grammatical changes which would clarify the client's statements
   C. make all grammatical changes so that the testimony is in standard English form
   D. ask the client's permission before making any grammatical changes

10. When the material typed on a printed form does not fill the space provided, a Z-ruling is frequently drawn to fill up the unused space.
    The MAIN purpose of this practice is to

    A. make the document more pleasing to the eye
    B. indicate that the preceding material is correct
    C. insure that the document is not altered
    D. show that the lawyer has read it

11. After you had typed an original and five copies of a certain document, some changes were made in ink on the original and were initialed by all the parties. The original was signed by all the parties, and the signatures were notarized.
    Which of the following should *generally* be typed on the copies BEFORE filing the original and the copies? The inked changes

    A. but not the signatures, initials, or notarial data
    B. the signatures and the initials but not the notarial data
    C. and the notarial data but not the signatures or initials
    D. the signatures, the initials, and the notarial data

12. The first paragraph of a noncourt agreement *generally* contains all of the following EXCEPT the

    A. specific terms of the agreement
    B. date of the agreement
    C. purpose of the agreement
    D. names of the parties involved

13. When typing an answer in a court proceeding, the place where the word ANSWER should be typed on the first page of the document is

    A. at the upper left-hand corner
    B. below the index number and to the right of the box containing the names of the parties to the action
    C. above the index number and to the right of the box containing the names of the parties to the action
    D. to the left of the names of the attorneys for the defendant

14. Which one of the following statements BEST describes the legal document called an acknowledgment?
    It is

    A. an answer to an affidavit
    B. a receipt issued by the court when a document is filed
    C. proof of service of a summons
    D. a declaration that a signature is valid

15. Suppose you typed the original and three copies of a legal document which was dictated by an attorney in your office. He has already signed the original copy, and corrections have been made on all copies.
    Regarding the copies, which one of the following procedures is the PROPER one to follow?

    A. Leave the signature line blank on the copies
    B. Ask the attorney to sign the copies
    C. Print or type the attorney's name on the signature line on the copies
    D. Sign your name to the copies followed by the attorney's initials

16. Suppose your office is defending a particular person in a court action. This person comes to the office and asks to see some of the lawyer's working papers in his file. The lawyer assigned to the case is out of the office at the time.
    You SHOULD

    A. permit him to examine his entire file as long as he does not remove any materials from it
    B. make an appointment for the caller to come back later when the lawyer will be there
    C. ask him what working papers he wants to see and show him only those papers
    D. tell him that he needs written permission from the lawyer in order to see any records

17. Suppose that you receive a phone call from an official who is annoyed about a letter from your office which she just received. The lawyer who dictated the letter is not in the office at the moment.
Of the following, the BEST action for you to take is to

    A. explain that the lawyer is out but that you will ask the lawyer to return her call when he returns
    B. take down all of the details of her complaint and tell her that you will get back to her with an explanation
    C. refer to the proper file so that you can give her an explanation of the reasons for the letter over the phone
    D. make an appointment for her to stop by the office to speak with the lawyer

18. Suppose that you have taken dictation for an interoffice memorandum. You are asked to prepare it for distribution to four lawyers in your department whose names are given to you. You will type an original and make four copies. Which one of the following is CORRECT with regard to the typing of the lawyers' names?
The names of all of the lawyers should appear

    A. *only* on the original
    B. on the original and each copy should have the name of one lawyer
    C. on each of the copies but not on the original
    D. on the original and on all of the copies

19. Regarding the correct typing of punctuation, the GENERALLY accepted practice is that there should be

    A. two spaces after a semi-colon
    B. one space before an apostrophe used in the body of a word
    C. no space between parentheses and the matter enclosed
    D. one space before and after a hyphen

20. Suppose you have just completed typing an original and two copies of a letter requesting information. The original is to be signed by a lawyer in your office. The first copy is for the files, and the second is to be used as a reminder to follow up.
The PROPER time to file the file copy of the letter is

    A. after the letter has been signed and corrections have been made on the copies
    B. before you take the letter to the lawyer for his signature
    C. after a follow-up letter has been sent
    D. after a response to the letter has been received

21. A secretary in a legal office has just typed a letter. She has typed the copy distribution notation on the copies to indicate *blind copy distribution*. This *blind copy* notation shows that

    A. copies of the letter are being sent to persons that the addressee does not know
    B. copies of the letter are being sent to other persons without the addressee's knowledge
    C. a copy of the letter will be enlarged for a legally blind person
    D. a copy of the letter is being given as an extra copy to the addressee

22. Suppose that one of the attorneys in your office dictates material to you without indicating punctuation. He has asked that you give him, as soon as possible, a single copy of a rough draft to be triple-spaced so that he can make corrections.
Of the following, what is the BEST thing for you to do in this situation?

   A. Assume that no punctuation is desired in the material
   B. Insert the punctuation as you type the rough draft
   C. Transcribe the material exactly as dictated, but attach a note to the attorney stating your suggested changes
   D. Before you start to type the draft, tell the attorney you want to read back your notes so that he can indicate punctuation

23. When it is necessary to type a mailing notation such as CERTIFIED, REGISTERED, or FEDEX on an envelope, the GENERALLY accepted place to type it is

   A. directly above the address
   B. in the area below where the stamp will be affixed
   C. in the lower left-hand corner
   D. in the upper left-hand corner

24. When taking a citation of a case in shorthand, which of the following should you write FIRST if you are having difficulty keeping up with the dictation?

   A. Volume and page number
   B. Title of volume
   C. Name of plaintiff
   D. Name of defendant

25. All of the following abbreviations and their meanings are correctly paired EXCEPT

   A. viz. - namely
   B. ibid. - refer
   C. n.b. - note well
   D. q.v. - which see

## KEY (CORRECT ANSWERS)

| | | | |
|---|---|---|---|
| 1. | D | 11. | D |
| 2. | D | 12. | A |
| 3. | B | 13. | B |
| 4. | B | 14. | D |
| 5. | A | 15. | C |
| 6. | C | 16. | B |
| 7. | D | 17. | A |
| 8. | A | 18. | D |
| 9. | A | 19. | C |
| 10. | C | 20. | A |

21. B
22. B
23. B
24. A
25. B

# PREPARING WRITTEN MATERIAL
# EXAMINATION SECTION
# TEST 1

DIRECTIONS: Each question or incomplete statement is followed by several suggested answers or completions. Select the one that BEST answers the question or completes the statement. *PRINT THE LETTER OF THE CORRECT ANSWER IN THE SPACE AT THE RIGHT.*

1. The one of the following sentences which is LEAST acceptable from the viewpoint of correct usage is:
    A. The police thought the fugitive to be him.
    B. The criminals set a trap for whoever would fall into it.
    C. It is ten years ago since the fugitive fled from the city.
    D. The lecturer argued that criminals are usually cowards.
    E. The police removed four bucketfuls of earth from the scene of the crime.

1.____

2. The one of the following sentences which is LEAST acceptable from the viewpoint of correct usage is:
    A. The patrolman scrutinized the report with great care.
    B. Approaching the victim of the assault, two bruises were noticed by the patrolman.
    C. As soon as I had broken down the door, I stepped into the room.
    D. I observed the accused loitering near the building, which was closed at the time.
    E. The storekeeper complained that his neighbor was guilty of violating a local ordinance.

2.____

3. The one of the following sentences which is LEAST acceptable from the viewpoint of correct usage is:
    A. I realized immediately that he intended to assault the woman, so I disarmed him.
    B. It was apparent that Mr. Smith's explanation contained many inconsistencies.
    C. Despite the slippery condition of the street, he managed to stop the vehicle before injuring the child.
    D. Not a single one of them wish, despite the damage to property, to make a formal complaint.
    E. The body was found lying on the floor.

3.____

4. The one of the following sentences which contains NO error in usage is:
    A. After the robbers left, the proprietor stood tied in his chair for about two hours before help arrived.
    B. In the cellar I found the watchman's hat and coat.
    C. The persons living in adjacent apartments stated that they had heard no unusual noises.

4.____

D. Neither a knife or any firearms were found in the room.
E. Walking down the street, the shouting of the crowd indicated that something was wrong.

5. The one of the following sentences which contains NO error in usage is:
    A. The policeman lay a firm hand on the suspect's shoulder.
    B. It is true that neither strength nor agility are the most important requirement for a good patrolman.
    C. Good citizens constantly strive to do more than merely comply the restraints imposed by society.
    D. No decision was made as to whom the prize should be awarded.
    E. Twenty years is considered a severe sentence for a felony.

6. Which of the following sentences is NOT expressed in standard English usage?
    A. The victim reached a pay-phone booth and manages to call police headquarters.
    B. By the time the call was received, the assailant had left the scene.
    C. The victim has been a respected member of the community for the past eleven years.
    D. Although the lighting was bad and the shadows were deep, the storekeeper caught sight of the attacker.
    E. Additional street lights have since been installed, and the patrols have been strengthened.

7. Which of the following sentences is NOT expressed in standard English usage?
    A. The judge upheld the attorney's right to question the witness about the missing glove.
    B. To be absolutely fair to all parties is the jury's chief responsibility.
    C. Having finished the report, a loud noise in the next room startled the sergeant.
    D. The witness obviously enjoyed having played a part in the proceedings.
    E. The sergeant planned to assign the case to whoever arrived first.

8. In which of the following sentences is a word misused?
    A. As a matter of principle, the captain insisted that the suspect's partner be brought for questioning.
    B. The principle suspect had been detained at the station house for most of the day.
    C. The principal in the crime had no previous criminal record, but his closest associate had been convicted of felonies on two occasions.
    D. The interest payments had been made promptly, but the firm had been drawing upon the principal for these payments.
    E. The accused insisted that his high school principal would furnish him a character reference.

3 (#1)

9. Which of the following statements is ambiguous?   9.____
   A. Mr. Sullivan explained why Mr. Johnson had been dismissed from his job.
   B. The storekeeper told the patrolman he had made a mistake.
   C. After waiting three hours, the patients in the doctor's office were sent home.
   D. The janitor's duties were to maintain the building in good shape and to answer tenants' complaints.
   E. The speed limit should, in my opinion, be raised to sixty miles an hour on that stretch of road.

10. In which of the following is the punctuation or capitalization faulty?   10.____
    A. The accident occurred at an intersection in the Kew Gardens section of Queens, near the bus stop.
    B. The sedan, not the convertible, was struck in the side.
    C. Before any of the patrolmen had left the police car received an important message from headquarters.
    D. The dog that had been stolen was returned to his master, John Dempsey, who lived in East Village.
    E. The letter had been sent to 12 Hillside Terrace, Rutland, Vermont 05702.

Questions 11-25.

DIRECTIONS: Questions 11 through 25 are to be answered in accordance with correct English usage; that is, standard English rather than nonstandard or substandard. Nonstandard and substandard English includes words or expressions usually classified as slang, dialect, illiterate, etc., which are not generally accepted as correct in current written communication. Standard English also requires clarity, proper punctuation and capitalization and appropriate use of words. Write the letter of the sentence NOT expressed in standard English usage in the space at the right.

11. A. There were three witnesses to the accident.   11.____
    B. At least three witnesses were found to testify for the plaintiff.
    C. Three of the witnesses who took the stand was uncertain about the defendant's competence to drive.
    D. Only three witnesses came forward to testify for the plaintiff.
    E. The three witnesses to the accident were pedestrians.

12. A. The driver had obviously drunk too many martinis before leaving for home.   12.____
    B. The boy who drowned had swum in these same waters many times before.
    C. The petty thief had stolen a bicycle from a private driveway before he was apprehended.
    D. The detectives had brung in the heroin shipment they intercepted.
    E. The passengers had never ridden in a converted bus before.

13. A. Between you and me, the new platoon plan sounds like a good idea.  13.____
    B. Money from an aunt's estate was left to his wife and he.
    C. He and I were assigned to the same patrol for the first time in two months.
    D. Either you or he should check the front door of that store.
    E. The captain himself was not sure of the witness's reliability.

14. A. The alarm had scarcely begun to ring when the explosion occurred.  14.____
    B. Before the firemen arrived at the scene, the second story had been destroyed.
    C. Because of the dense smoke and heat, the firemen could hardly approach the now-blazing structure.
    D. According to the patrolman's report, there wasn't nobody in the store when the explosion occurred.
    E. The sergeant's suggestion was not at all unsound, but no one agreed with him.

15. A. The driver and the passenger they were both found to be intoxicated.  15.____
    B. The driver and the passenger talked slowly and not too clearly.
    C. Neither the driver nor his passengers were able to give a coherent account of the accident.
    D. In a corner of the room sat the passenger, quietly dozing.
    E. the driver finally told a strange and unbelievable story, which the passenger contradicted.

16. A. Under the circumstances I decided not to continue my examination of the premises.  16.____
    B. There are many difficulties now not comparable with those existing in 1960.
    C. Friends of the accused were heard to announce that the witness had better been away on the day of the trial.
    D. The two criminals escaped in the confusion that followed the explosion.
    E. The aged man was struck by the considerateness of the patrolman's offer.

17. A. An assemblage of miscellaneous weapons lay on the table.  17.____
    B. Ample opportunities were given to the defendant to obtain counsel.
    C. The speaker often alluded to his past experience with youthful offenders in the armed forces.
    D. The sudden appearance of the truck aroused my suspicions.
    E. Her studying had a good affect on her grades in high school.

18. A. He sat down in the theater and began to watch the movie.  18.____
    B. The girl had ridden horses since she was four years old.
    C. Application was made on behalf of the prosecutor to cite the witness for contempt.
    D. The bank robber, with his two accomplices, were caught in the act.
    E. His story is simply not credible.

19.  A. The angry boy said that he did not like those kind of friends.
     B. The merchant's financial condition was so precarious that he felt he must avail himself of any offer of assistance.
     C. He is apt to promise more than he can perform.
     D. Looking at the messy kitchen, the housewife felt like crying.
     E. A clerk was left in charge of the stolen property.

20.  A. His wounds were aggravated by prolonged exposure to sub-freezing temperatures.
     B. The prosecutor remarked that the witness was not averse to changing his story each time he was interviewed.
     C. The crime pattern indicated that the burglars were adapt in the handling of explosives.
     D. His rigid adherence to a fixed plan brought him into renewed conflict with his subordinates.
     E. He had anticipated that the sentence would be delivered by noon.

21.  A. The whole arraignment procedure is badly in need of revision.
     B. After his glasses were broken in the fight, he would of gone to the optometrist if he could.
     C. Neither Tom nor Jack brought his lunch to work.
     D. He stood aside until the quarrel was over.
     E. A statement in the psychiatrist's report disclosed that the probationer vowed to have his revenge.

22.  A. His fiery and intemperate speech to the striking employees fatally affected any chance of a future reconciliation.
     B. The wording of the statute has been variously construed.
     C. The defendant's attorney, speaking in the courtroom, called the official a demagogue who contempuously disregarded the judge's orders.
     D. The baseball game is likely to be the most exciting one this year.
     E. The mother divided the cookies among her two children.

23.  A. There was only a bed and a dresser in the dingy room.
     B. John was one of the few students that have protested the new rule.
     C. It cannot be argued that the child's testimony is negligible; it is, on the contrary, of the greatest importance.
     D. The basic criterion for clearance was so general that officials resolved any doubts in favor of dismissal.
     E. Having just returned from a long vacation, the officer found the city unbearably hot.

24.  A. The librarian ought to give more help to small children.
     B. The small boy was criticized by the teacher because he often wrote careless.
     C. It was generally doubted whether the women would permit the use of her apartment for intelligence operations.
     D. The probationer acts differently every time the officer visits him.
     E. Each of the newly appointed officers has 12 years of service.

25.
- A. The North is the most industrialized region in the country.
- B. L. Patrick Gray 3d, the bureau's acting director, stated that, while "rehabilitation is fine" for some convicted criminals, "it is a useless gesture for those who resist every such effort."
- C. Careless driving, faulty mechanism, narrow or badly kept roads all play their part in causing accidents.
- D. The childrens' books were left in the bus.
- E. It was a matter of internal security; consequently, he felt no inclination to rescind his previous order.

## KEY (CORRECT ANSWERS)

| | | | | |
|---|---|---|---|---|
| 1. | C | | 11. | C |
| 2. | B | | 12. | D |
| 3. | D | | 13. | B |
| 4. | C | | 14. | D |
| 5. | E | | 15. | A |
| 6. | A | | 16. | C |
| 7. | C | | 17. | E |
| 8. | B | | 18. | D |
| 9. | B | | 19. | A |
| 10. | C | | 20. | C |

| | |
|---|---|
| 21. | B |
| 22. | E |
| 23. | B |
| 24. | B |
| 25. | D |

# TEST 2

DIRECTIONS: Each question or incomplete statement is followed by several suggested answers or completions. Select the one that BEST answers the question or completes the statement. *PRINT THE LETTER OF THE CORRECT ANSWER IN THE SPACE AT THE RIGHT.*

Questions 1-6.

DIRECTIONS: Each of Questions 1 through 6 consists of a statement which contains a word (one of those underlined) that is either incorrectly used because it is not in keeping with the meaning the quotation is evidently intended to convey, or is misspelled. There is only one INCORRECT word in each quotation. Of the four underlined words, determine if the first one should be replaced by the word lettered A, the second replaced by the word lettered B, the third replaced by the word lettered C, or the fourth replaced by the word lettered D.

1. Whether one depends on <u>fluorescent</u> or artificial light or both, adequate <u>standards</u> should be <u>maintained</u> by means of <u>systematic</u> tests.  1.____
   A. natural   B. safeguards   C. established   D. routine

2. A police officer has to be <u>prepared</u> to assume his <u>knowledge</u> as a social <u>scientist</u> in the <u>community</u>.  2.____
   A. forced   B. role   C. philosopher   D. street

3. It is <u>practically</u> impossible to <u>indicate</u> whether a sentence is <u>too</u> long simply by <u>measuring</u> its length.  3.____
   A. almost   B. tell   C. very   D. guessing

4. Strong <u>leaders</u> are <u>required</u> to organize a community for delinquency prevention and for <u>dissemination</u> of organized <u>crime</u> and drug addiction.  4.____
   A. tactics   B. important   C. control   D. meetings

5. The <u>demonstrators</u> who were taken to the Criminal Courts building in <u>Manhattan</u> (because it was large enough to <u>accommodate</u> them), contended that the arrests were <u>unwarranted</u>.  5.____
   A. demonstraters         B. Manhatten
   C. accomodate            D. unwarranted

6. They were <u>guaranteed</u> a calm <u>atmosphere</u>, free from <u>harassment</u>, which would be conducive to quiet consideration of the <u>indictments</u>.  6.____
   A. guarenteed            B. atmspher
   C. harassment            D. inditements

Questions 7-11.

DIRECTIONS: Each of Questions 7 through 11 consists of a statement containing four words in capital letters. One of these words in capital letters is not in keeping with the meaning which the statement is evidently intended to carry. The four words in capital letters in each statement are reprinted after the statement. Print the capital letter preceding the one of the four words which does MOST to spoil the true meaning of the statement in the space at the right.

7. Retirement and pension systems are essential not only to provide employees with with a means of support in the future, but also to prevent longevity and CHARITABLE considerations from UPSETTING the PROMOTIONAL opportunities RETIRED members of the career service.
   A. charitable   B. upsetting   C. promotional   D. retired

7.____

8. Within each major DIVISION in a properly set up public or private organization, provision is made so that each NECESSARY activity is CARED for and lines of authority and responsibility are clear-cut and INFINITE.
   A. division   B. necessary   C. cared   D. infinite

8.____

9. In public service, the scale of salaries paid must be INCIDENTAL to the services rendered, with due CONSIDERATION for the attraction of the desired MANPOWER and for the maintenance of a standard of living COMMENSURATE with the work to be performed.
   A. incidental         B. consideration
   C. manpower         D. commensurate

9.____

10. An understanding of the AIMS of an organization by the staff will AID greatly in increasing the DEMAND of the correspondence work of the office, and will to a large extent DETERMINE the nature of the correspondence.
    A. aims   B. aid   C. demand   D. determine

10.____

11. BECAUSE the Civil Service Commission strongly feels that the MERIT system is a key factor in the MAINTENANCE of democratic government, it has adopted as one of its major DEFENSES the progressive democratization of its own procedures in dealing with candidates for positions in the public service.
    A. Because   B. merit   C. maintenance   D. defenses

11.____

Questions 12-14.

DIRECTIONS: Questions 12 through 14 consist of one sentence each. Each sentence contains an incorrectly used word. First, decide which is the incorrectly used word. Then, from among the options given, decide which word, when substituted for the incorrectly used word, makes the meaning of the sentence clear.
EXAMPLE:
The U.S. national income exhibits a pattern of long term deflection.
   A. reflection   B. subjection   C. rejoicing   D. growth

The word *deflection* in the sentence does not convey the meaning the sentence evidently intended to convey. The word *growth* (Answer D), when substituted for the word *deflection*, makes the meaning of the sentence clear. Accordingly, the answer to the question is D.

12. The study commissioned by the joint committee fell compassionately short of the mark and would have to be redone.
    A. successfully        B. insignificantly
    C. experimentally      D. woefully

13. He will not idly exploit any violation of the provisions of the order.
    A. tolerate    B. refuse    C. construe    D. guard

14. The defendant refused to be virile and bitterly protested service.
    A. irked    B. feasible    C. docile    D. credible

Questions 15-25.

DIRECTIONS: Questions 15 through 25 consist of short paragraphs. Each paragraph contains one word which is INCORRECTLY used because it is NOT in keeping with the meaning of the paragraph. Find the word in each paragraph which is INCORRECTLY used and then select as the answer the suggested word which should be substituted for the incorrectly used word.

SAMPLE QUESTION:
In determining who is to do the work in your unit, you will have to decide just who does what from day to day. One of your lowest responsibilities is to assign work so that everybody gets a fair share and that everyone can do his part well.
   A. new    B. old    C. important    D. performance

EXPLANATION:
The word which is NOT in keeping with the meaning of the paragraph is *lowest*. This is the INCORRECTLY used word. The suggested word *important* would be in keeping with the meaning of the paragraph and should be substituted for *lowest*. Therefore, the CORRECT answer is choice C.

15. If really good practice in the elimination of preventable injuries is to be achieved and held in any establishment, top management must refuse full and definite responsibility and must apply a good share of its attention to the task.
    A. accept    B. avoidable    C. duties    D. problem

16. Recording the human face for identification is by no means the only service performed by the camera in the field of investigation. When the trial of any issue takes place, a word picture is sought to be distorted to the court of incidents, occurrences, or events which are in dispute.
    A. appeals    B. description    C. portrayed    D. deranged

4 (#2)

17. In the collection of physical evidence, it cannot be emphasized too strongly that a haphazard systematic search at the scene of the crime is vital. Nothing must be overlooked. Often the only leads in a case will come from the results of this search.
    A. important  B. investigation
    C. proof      D. thorough

17.____

18. If an investigator has reason to suspect that the witness is mentally stable, or a habitual drunkard, he should leave no stone unturned in his investigation to determine if the witness was under the influence of liquor or drugs, or was mentally unbalanced either at the time of the occurrence to which he testified or at the time of the trial.
    A. accused    B. clue    C. deranged    D. question

18.____

19. The use of records is a valuable step in crime investigation and is the main reason every department should maintain accurate reports. Crimes are not committed through the use of departmental records alone but from the use of all records, of almost every type, wherever they may be found and whenever they give any incidental information regarding the criminal.
    A. accidental    B. necessary    C. reported    D. solved

19.____

20. In the years since passage of the Harrison Narcotic Act of 1914, making the possession of opium amphetamines illegal in most circumstances, drug use has become a subject of considerable scientific interest and investigation. There is at present a voluminous literature on drug use of various kinds.
    A. ingestion    B. derivatives    C. addiction    D. opiates

20.____

21. Of course, the fact that criminal laws are extremely patterned in definition does not mean that the majority of persons who violate them are dealt with as criminals. Quite the contrary, for a great many forbidden acts are voluntarily engaged in within situations of privacy and go unobserved and unreported.
    A. symbolic    B. casual    C. scientific    D. broad-gauged

21.____

22. The most punitive way to study punishment is to focus attention on the pattern of punitive action: to study how a penalty is applied, too study what is done to or taken from an offender.
    A. characteristic    B. degrading    C. objective    D. distinguished

22.____

23. The most common forms of punishment in times past have been death, physical torture, mutilation, branding, public humiliation, fines, forfeits of property, banishment, transportation, and imprisonment. Although this list is by no means differentiated, practically every form of punishment has had several variations and applications.
    A. specific    B. simple    C. exhaustive    D. characteristic

23.____

24. There is another important line of inference between ordinary and professional criminals, and that is the source from which they are recruited. The professional criminal seems to be drawn from legitimate employment and, in many instances, from parallel vocations or pursuits.  24.____
    A. demarcation   B. justification   C. superiority   D. reference

25. He took the position that the success of the program was insidious on getting additional revenue.  25.____
    A. reputed   B. contingent   C. failure   D. indeterminate

## KEY (CORRECT ANSWERS)

| | | | | |
|---|---|---|---|---|
| 1. | A | | 11. | D |
| 2. | B | | 12. | D |
| 3. | B | | 13. | A |
| 4. | C | | 14. | C |
| 5. | D | | 15. | A |
| 6. | C | | 16. | C |
| 7. | D | | 17. | D |
| 8. | D | | 18. | C |
| 9. | A | | 19. | D |
| 10. | C | | 20. | B |

| | |
|---|---|
| 21. | D |
| 22. | C |
| 23. | C |
| 24. | A |
| 25. | B |

# TEST 3

DIRECTIONS: Each question or incomplete statement is followed by several suggested answers or completions. Select the one that BEST answers the question or completes the statement. *PRINT THE LETTER OF THE CORRECT ANSWER IN THE SPACE AT THE RIGHT.*

Questions 1-5.

DIRECTIONS: Questions 1 through 5 are to be answered on the basis of the following.

You are a supervising officer in an investigative unit. Earlier in the day, you directed Detectives Tom Dixon and Sal Mayo to investigate a reported assault and robbery in a liquor store within your area of jurisdiction.

Detective Dixon has submitted to you a preliminary investigative report containing the following information:

- At 1630 hours on 2/20, arrived at Joe's Liquor Store at 350 SW Avenue with Detective Mayo to investigate A & R.
- At store interviewed Rob Ladd, store manager, who stated that he and Joe Brown (store owner) had been stuck up about ten minutes prior to our arrival.
- Ladd described the robbers as male whites in their late teens or early twenties. Further stated that one of the robbers displayed what appeared to be an automatic pistol as he entered the store, and said, *Give us the money or we'll kill you.* Ladd stated that Brown then reached under the counter where he kept a loaded .38 caliber pistol. Several shots followed, and Ladd threw himself to the floor.
- The robbers fled, and Ladd didn't know if any money had been taken.
- At this point, Ladd realized that Brown was unconscious on the floor and bleeding from a head wound.
- Ambulance called by Ladd, and Brown was removed by same to General Hospital.
- Personally interviewed John White, 382 Dartmouth Place, who stated he was inside store at the time of occurrence. White states that he hid behind a wine display upon hearing someone say, *Give us the money.* He then heard shots and saw two young men run from the store to a yellow car parked at the curb. White was unable to further describe auto. States the taller of the two men drove the car away while the other sat on passenger side in front.
- Recovered three spent .38 caliber bullets from premises and delivered them to Crime Lab.
- To General Hospital at 1800 hours but unable to interview Brown, who was under sedation and suffering from shock and a laceration of the head.
- Alarm #12487 transmitted for car and occupants.
- Case Active.

Based solely on the contents of the preliminary investigation submitted by Detective Dixon, select one sentence from the following groups of sentences which is MOST accurate and is grammatically correct.

1.  A. Both robbers were armed.
    B. Each of the robbers were described as a male white.
    C. Neither robber was armed.
    D. Mr. Ladd stated that one of the robbers was armed.

    1.____

2.  A. Mr. Brown fired three shots from his revolver.
    B. Mr. Brown was shot in the head by one of the robbers.
    C. Mr. Brown suffered a gunshot wound of the head during the course of the robbery.
    D. Mr. Brown was taken to General Hospital by ambulance.

    2.____

3.  A. Shots were fired after one of the robbers said, *Give us the money or we'll kill you.*
    B. After one of the robbers demanded the money from Mr. Brown, he fired a shot.
    C. The preliminary investigation indicated that although Mr. Brown did not have a license for the gun, he was justified in using deadly physical force.
    D. Mr. Brown was interviewed at General Hospital.

    3.____

4.  A. Each of the witnesses were customers in the store at the time of occurrence.
    B. Neither of the witnesses interviewed was the owner of the liquor store.
    C. Neither of the witnesses interviewed were the owner of the store.
    D. Neither of the witnesses was employed by Mr. Brown.

    4.____

5.  A. Mr. Brown arrived at General Hospital at about 5:00 P.M.
    B. Neither of the robbers was injured during the robbery.
    C. The robbery occurred at 3:30 P.M. on February 10.
    D. One of the witnesses called the ambulance.

    5.____

Questions 6-10.

DIRECTIONS:  Each of Questions 6 through 10 consists of information given in outline form and four sentences labeled A, B, C, and D.  For each question, choose the one sentence which CORRECTLY expresses the information given in outline form and which also displays PROPER English usage.

6.  Client's Name:  Joanna Jones
    Number of Children:  3
    Client's Income:  None
    Client's Marital Status:  Single

    A. Joanna Jones is an unmarried client with three children who have no income.
    B. Joanna Jones, who is single and has no income, a client she has three children.
    C. Joanna Jones, whose three children are clients, is single and has no income.
    D. Joanna Jones, who has three children, is an unmarried client with no income.

    6.____

7. Client's Name: Bertha Smith
   Number of Children: 2
   Client's Rent: $1050 per month
   Number of Rooms: 4

   A. Bertha Smith, a client, pays $1050 per month for her four rooms with two children.
   B. Client Bertha Smith has two children and pays $1050 per month for four rooms.
   C. Client Bertha Smith is paying $1050 per month for two children with four rooms.
   D. For four rooms and two children client Bertha Smith pays $1050 per month.

7.____

8. Name of Employee: Cynthia Dawes
   Number of Cases Assigned: 9
   Date Cases were Assigned: 12/16
   Number of Assigned Cases Completed: 8

   A. On December 16, employee Cynthia Dawes was assigned nine cases; she has completed eight of these cases.
   B. Cynthia Dawes, employee on December 16, assigned nine cases, completed eight.
   C. Being employed on December 16, Cynthia Dawes completed eight of nine assigned cases.
   D. Employee Cynthia Dawes, she was assigned nine cases and completed eight, on December 16.

8.____

9. Place of Audit: Broadway Center
   Names of Auditors: Paul Cahn, Raymond Perez
   Date of Audit: 11/20
   Number of Cases Audited: 41

   A. On November 20, at the Broadway Center 41 cases was audited by auditors Paul Cahn and Raymond Perez.
   B. Auditors Raymond Perez and Paul Cahn has audited 41 cases at the Broadway Center on November 20.
   C. At the Broadway Center, on November 20, auditors Paul Cahn and Raymond Perez audited 41 cases.
   D. Auditors Paul Cahn and Raymond Perez at the Broadway Center, on November 20, is auditing 41 cases.

9.____

10. Name of Client: Barbra Levine
    Client's Monthly Income: $2100
    Client's Monthly Expenses: $4520

    A. Barbra Levine is a client, her monthly income is $2100 and her monthly expenses is $4520.
    B. Barbra Levine's monthly income is $2100 and she is a client, with whose monthly expenses are $4520.

10.____

C. Barbra Levine is a client whose monthly income is $2100 and whose monthly expenses are $4520.
D. Barbra Levine, a client, is with a monthly income which is $2100 and monthly expenses which are $4520.

Questions 11-13.

DIRECTIONS: Questions 11 through 13 involve several statements of fact presented in a very simple way. These statements of fact are followed by 4 choices which attempt to incorporate all of the facts into one logical statement which is properly constructed and grammatically correct.

11. I. Mr. Brown was sweeping the sidewalk in front of his house.
    II. He was sweeping it because it was dirty.
    III. He swept the refuse into the street.
    IV. Police Officer gave him a ticket.

    Which one of the following BEST presents the information given above?
    A. Because his sidewalk was dirty, Mr. Brown received a ticket from Officer Green when he swept the refuse into the street.
    B. Police Officer Green gave Mr. Brown a ticket because his sidewalk was dirty and he swept the refuse into the street.
    C. Police Officer Green gave Mr. Brown a ticket for sweeping refuse into the street because his sidewalk was dirty.
    D. Mr. Brown, who was sweeping refuse from his dirty sidewalk into the street, was given a ticket by Police Officer Green.

12. I. Sergeant Smith radioed for help.
    II. The sergeant did so because the crowd was getting larger.
    III. It was 10:00 A.M. when he made his call.
    IV. Sergeant Smith was not in uniform at the time of occurrence.

    Which one of the following BEST presents the information given above?
    A. Sergeant Smith, although not on duty at the time, radioed for help at 10 o'clock because the crowd was getting uglier.
    B. Although not in uniform, Sergeant Smith called for help at 10:00 A.M. because the crowd was getting uglier.
    C. Sergeant Smith radioed for help at 10:00 A.M. because the crowd was getting larger.
    D. Although he was not in uniform, Sergeant Smith radioed for help at 10:00 A.M. because the crowd was getting larger.

13. I. The payroll office is open on Fridays.
    II. Paychecks are distributed from 9:00 A.M. to 12 Noon.
    III. The office is open on Fridays because that's the only day the payroll staff is available.
    IV. It is open for the specified hours in order to permit employees to cash checks at the bank during lunch hour.

The choice below which MOST clearly and accurately presents the above idea is:
- A. Because the payroll office is open on Fridays from 9:00 A.M. to 12 Noon, employees can cash their checks when the payroll staff is available.
- B. Because the payroll staff is only available on Fridays until noon, employees can cash their checks during their lunch hour.
- C. Because the payroll staff is available only on Fridays, the office is open from 9:00 A.M. to 12 Noon to allow employees to cash their checks.
- D. Because of payroll staff availability, the payroll office is open on Fridays. It is open from 9:00 A.M. to 12 Noon so that distributed paychecks can be cashed at the bank while employees are on their lunch hour.

Questions 14-16.

DIRECTIONS: In each of Questions 14 through 6, the four sentences are from a paragraph in a report. They are not in the right order. Which of the following arrangements is the BEST one?

14.
  I. An executive may answer a letter by writing his reply on the face of the letter itself instead of having a return letter typed.
  II. This procedure is efficient because it saves the executive's time, the typist's time, and saves office file space.
  III. Copying machines are used in small offices as well as large offices to save time and money in making brief replies to business letters.
  IV. A copy is made on a copy machine to go into the company files, while the original is mailed back to the sender.

  The CORRECT answer is:
  A. I, II, IV, III    B. I, IV, II, III    C. III, I, IV, II    D. III, IV, II, I

14.____

15.
  I. Most organizations favor one of the types but always include the others to a lesser degree.
  II. However, we can detect a definite trend toward greater use of symbolic control.
  III. We suggest that our local police agencies are today primarily utilizing material control.
  IV. Control can be classified into three types: physical, material, and symbolic.

  The CORRECT answer is:
  A. IV, II, III, I    B. II, I, IV, III    C. III, IV, II, I    D. IV, I, III, II

15.____

16.
  I. They can and do take advantage of ancient political and geographical boundaries, which often give them sanctuary from effective policy activity.
  II. This country is essentially a country of small police forces, each operating independently within the limits of its jurisdiction.
  III. The boundaries that define and limit police operations do not hinder the movement of criminals, of course.
  IV. The machinery of law enforcement in America is fragmented, complicated, and frequently overlapping.

16.____

The CORRECT answer is:
A. III, I, IV   B. II, IV, I, III   C. IV, II, III, I   D. IV, III, II, I

17. Examine the following sentence, and then choose from below the words which should be inserted in the blank spaces to produce the best sentence.
The unit has exceeded _____ goals and the employees are satisfied with _____ accomplishments.
A. their, it's   B. it's; it's   C. its, there   D. its, their

18. Examine the following sentence, and then choose from below the words which should be inserted in the blank spaces to produce the best sentence.
Research indicates that employees who _____ no opportunity for close social relationships often find their work unsatisfying, and this _____ of satisfaction often reflects itself in low production.
A. have; lack   B. have; excess   C. has; lack   D. has; excess

19. Words in a sentence must be arranged properly to make sure that the intended meaning of the sentence is clear.
The sentence below that does NOT make sense because a clause has been separated from the word on which its meaning depends is:
A. To be a good writer, clarity is necessary.
B. To be a good writer, you must write clearly.
C. You must write clearly to be a good writer.
D. Clarity is necessary to good writing.

Questions 20-21.

DIRECTIONS: Each of Questions 20 and 21 consists of a statement which contains a word (one of those underlined) that is either incorrectly used because it is not in keeping with the meaning the quotation is evidently intended to convey, or is misspelled. There is only one INCORRECT word in each quotation. Of the four underlined words, determine if the first one should be replaced by the word lettered A, the second one replaced by the word lettered B, the third one replaced by the word lettered C, or the fourth one replaced by the word lettered D.

20. The alleged killer was occasionally permitted to excercise in the corridor.
A. alledged   B. ocasionally   C. permited   D. exercise

21. Defense counsel stated, in affect, that their conduct was permissible under the First Amendment.
A. council   B. effect   C. there   D. permissable

Question 22.

DIRECTIONS: Question 22 consists of one sentence. This sentence contains an incorrectly used word. First, decide which is the incorrectly used word. Then, from among the options given, decide which word, when substituted for the incorrectly used word, makes the meaning of the sentence clear.

22. As today's violence has no single cause, so its causes have no single scheme.  22._____
    A. deference    B. cure    C. flaw    D. relevance

23. In the sentence, *A man in a light-grey suit waited thirty-five minutes in the ante-room for the all-important document*, the word IMPROPERLY hyphenated is  23._____
    A. light-grey
    B. thirty-five
    C. ante-room
    D. all-important

24. In the sentence, *The candidate wants to file his application for preference before it is too late*, the word *before* is used as a(n)  24._____
    A. preposition
    B. subordinating conjunction
    C. pronoun
    D. adverb

25. In the sentence, *The perpetrators ran from the scene*, the word *from* is a  25._____
    A. preposition    B. pronoun    C. verb    D. conjunction

## KEY (CORRECT ANSWERS)

| | | | |
|---|---|---|---|
| 1. | D | 11. | D |
| 2. | D | 12. | D |
| 3. | A | 13. | D |
| 4. | B | 14. | C |
| 5. | D | 15. | D |
| 6. | D | 16. | C |
| 7. | B | 17. | D |
| 8. | A | 18. | A |
| 9. | C | 19. | A |
| 10. | C | 20. | D |

21. B
22. B
23. C
24. B
25. A

# PREPARING WRITTEN MATERIAL

## PARAGRAPH REARRANGEMENT
## COMMENTARY

The sentences that follow are in scrambled order. You are to rearrange them in proper order and indicate the letter choice containing the correct answer at the space at the right.

Each group of sentences in this section is actually a paragraph presented in scrambled order. Each sentence in the group has a place in that paragraph; no sentence is to be left out. You are to read each group of sentences and decide upon the best order in which to put the sentences so as to form a well-organized paragraph.

The questions in this section measure the ability to solve a problem when all the facts relevant to its solution are not given.

More specifically, certain positions of responsibility and authority require the employee to discover connection between events sometimes, apparently, unrelated. In order to do this, the employee will find it necessary to correctly infer that unspecified events have probably occurred or are likely to occur. This ability becomes especially important when action must be taken on incomplete information.

Accordingly, these questions require competitors to choose among several suggested alternatives, each of which presents a different sequential arrangement of the events. Competitors must choose the MOST logical of the suggested sequences.

In order to do so, they may be required to draw on general knowledge to infer missing concepts or events that are essential to sequencing the given events. Competitors should be careful to infer only what is essential to the sequence. The plausibility of the wrong alternatives will always require the inclusion of unlikely events or of additional chains of events which are NOT essential to sequencing the given events.

It's very important to remember that you are looking for the best of the four possible choices, and that the best choice of all may not even be one of the answers you're given to choose from.

There is no one right way to solve these problems. Many people have found it helpful to first write out the order of the sentences, as they would have arranged them, on their scrap paper before looking at the possible answers. If their optimum answer is there, this can save them some time. If it isn't, this method can still give insight into solving the problem. Others find it most helpful to just go through each of the possible choices, contrasting each as they go along. You should use whatever method feels comfortable and works for you.

While most of these types of questions are not that difficult, we've added a higher percentage of the difficult type, just to give you more practice. Usually there are only one or two questions on this section that contain such subtle distinctions that you're unable to answer confidently. And you then may find yourself stuck deciding between two possible choices, neither of which you're sure about.

# EXAMINATION SECTION
# TEST 1

DIRECTIONS: The sentences that follow are in scrambled order. You are to rearrange them in proper order and indicate the letter choice containing the correct answer. *PRINT THE LETTER OF THE CORRECT ANSWER IN THE SPACE AT THE RIGHT.*

1. Below are four statements labeled W, X, Y and Z.  1.____
   W. He was a strict and fanatic drillmaster.
   X. The word is always used in a derogatory sense and generally shows resentment and anger on the part of the user.
   Y. It is from the name of this Frenchman that we derive our English word, martinet.
   Z. Jean Martinet was the Inspector-General of Infantry during the reign of King Louis XIV.
   The PROPER order in which these sentences should be placed in a paragraph is:
   A. X, Z, W, Y     B. X, Z, Y, W     C. Z, W, Y, X     D. Z, Y, W, X

2. In the following paragraph, the sentences, which are numbered, have been jumbled.  2.____
   I. Since then it has undergone changes.
   II. It was incorporated in 1955 under the laws of the State of New York.
   III. Its primary purposes, a cleaner city, has, however, remained the same.
   IV. The Citizens Committee works in cooperation with the Mayor's Inter-departmental Committee for a Clean City.  3.____
   The order in which these sentences should be arranged to form a well-organized paragraph is:
   A. II, IV, I, III     B. III, IV, I, II     C. IV, II, I, III     D. IV, III, II, I

Questions 3-5.

DIRECTIONS: The sentences listed below are part of a meaningful paragraph but they are not given in their proper order. You are to decide what would be the BEST order in which to put the sentences so as to form a well-organized paragraph. Each sentence has a place in the paragraph; there are no extra sentences. You are then to answer Questions 3 through 5 inclusive on the basis of your rearrangements of these scrambled sentences into a properly organized paragraph.

In 1887 some insurance companies organized an Inspection Department to advise their clients on all phases of fire prevention and protection. Probably this has been due to the smaller annual fire losses in Great Britain than in the United States. It tests various fire prevention devices and appliances and determines manufacturing hazards and their safeguards. Fire research began earlier in the United States and is more advanced than in Great Britain. Later they established a laboratory specializing in electrical, mechanical, hydraulic, and chemical fields.

2 (#1)

3. When the five sentences are arranged in proper order, the paragraph starts with the sentence which begins
   A. "In 1887..."   B. "Probably this..."   C. "It tests..."
   D. "Fire research..."   E. "Later they..."

   3._____

4. In the last sentence listed above, "they" refers to
   A. the insurance companies   B. the United States and Great Britain
   C. the Inspection Department   D. clients
   E. technicians

   4._____

5. When the above paragraph is properly arranged, it ends with the words
   A. "...and protection."   B. "...the United States."
   C. "...their safeguards."   D. "...in Great Britain."
   E. "...chemical fields."

   5._____

## KEY (CORRECT ANSWERS)

1. C
2. C
3. D
4. A
5. C

# TEST 2

DIRECTIONS: In each of the questions numbered I through V, several sentences are given. For each question, choose as your answer the group of number that represents the MOST logical order of these sentences if they were arranged in paragraph form. *PRINT THE LETTER OF THE CORRECT ANSWER IN THE SPACE AT THE RIGHT.*

1. 
   I. It is established when one shows that the landlord has prevented the tenant's enjoyment of his interest in the property leased.
   II. Constructive eviction is the result of a breach of the covenant of quiet enjoyment implied in all leases.
   III. In some parts of the United States, it is not complete until the tenant vacates within a reasonable time.
   IV. Generally, the acts must be of such serious and permanent character as to deny the tenant the enjoyment of his possessing rights.
   V. In this event, upon abandonment of the premises, the tenant's liability for that ceases.
   The CORRECT answer is:
   A. II, I, IV, III, V
   B. V, II, III, I, IV
   C. IV, III, I, II, V
   D. I, III, V, IV, II

   1.____

2. 
   I. The powerlessness before private and public authorities that is the typical experience of the slum tenant is reminiscent of the situation of blue-collar workers all through the nineteenth century.
   II. Similarly, in recent years, this chapter of history has been reopened by anti-poverty groups which have attempted to organize slum tenants to enable them to bargain collectively with their landlords about the conditions of their tenancies.
   III. It is familiar history that many of the worker remedied their condition by joining together and presenting their demands collectively.
   IV. Like the workers, tenants are forced by the conditions of modern life into substantial dependence on these who possess great political aid and economic power.
   V. What's more, the very fact of dependence coupled with an absence of education and self-confidence makes them hesitant and unable to stand up for what they need from those in power.
   The CORRECT answer is:
   A. V, IV, I, II, III
   B. II, III, I, V, IV
   C. III, I, V, IV, II
   D. I, IV, V, III, II

   2.____

3. 
   I. A railroad, for example, when not acting as a common carrier may contract away responsibility for its own negligence.
   II. As to a landlord, however, no decision has been found relating to the legal effect of a clause shifting the statutory duty of repair to the tenant.
   III. The courts have not passed on the validity of clauses relieving the landlord of this duty and liability.
   IV. They have, however, upheld the validity of exculpatory clauses in other types of contracts.

   3.____

89

V. Housing regulations impose a duty upon the landlord to maintain leased premises in safe condition.
VI. As another example, a bailee may limit his liability except for gross negligence, willful acts, or fraud.
The CORRECT answer is:
A. II, I, VI, IV, III, V
B. I, III, IV, V, VI, II
C. III, V, I, IV, II, VI
D. V, III, IV, I, VI, II

4.  I. Since there are only samples in the building, retail or consumer sales are generally eschewed by mart occupants, and in some instances, rigid controls are maintained to limit entrance to the mart only to those persons engaged in retailing.
    II. Since World War I, in many larger cities, there has developed a new type of property, called the mart building.
    III. It can, therefore, be used by wholesalers and jobbers for the display of sample merchandise.
    IV. This type of building is most frequently a multi-storied, finished interior property which is a cross between a retail arcade and a loft building.
    V. This limitation enables the mart occupants to ship the orders from another location after the retailer or dealer makes his selection from the samples.
    The CORRECT answer is:
    A. II, IV, III, I, V
    B. IV, III, V, I, II
    C. I, III, II, IV, V
    D. I, IV, II, III, V

5.  I. In general, staff-line friction reduces the distinctive contribution of staff personnel.
    II. The conflicts, however, introduce an uncontrolled element into the managerial system.
    III. On the other hand, the natural resistance of the line to staff innovations probably usefully restrains over-eager efforts to apply untested procedures on a large scale.
    IV. Under such conditions, it is difficult to know when valuable ideas are being sacrificed.
    V. The relatively weak position of staff, requiring accommodation to the line, tends to restrict their ability to engage in free, experimental innovation.
    The CORRECT answer is:
    A. IV, II, III, I, V
    B. I, V, III, II, IV
    C. V, III, I, II, IV
    D. II, I, IV, V, III

## KEY (CORRECT ANSWERS)

1. A
2. D
3. D
4. A
5. B

# TEST 3

DIRECTIONS: Questions 1 through 4 consist of six sentences which can be arranged in a logical sequence. For each question, select the choice which places the numbered sentences in the MOST logical sequent. *PRINT THE LETTER OF THE CORRECT ANSWER IN THE SPACE AT THE RIGHT.*

1.  I. The burden of proof as to each issue is determined before trial and remains upon the same party throughout the trial.
    II. The jury is at liberty to believe one witness' testimony as against a number of contradictory witnesses.
    III. In a civil case, the party bearing the burden of proof is required to prove his contention by a fair preponderance of the evidence.
    IV. However, it must be noted that a fair preponderance of evidence does not necessarily mean a greater number of witnesses.
    V. The burden of proof is the burden which rests upon one of the parties to an action to persuade the trier of the facts, generally the jury, that a proposition he asserts is true.
    VI. If the evidence is equally balanced, or if it leaves the jury in such doubt as to be unable to decide the controversy either way, judgment must be given against the party upon whom the burden of proof rests.
    The CORRECT answer is:
    A. III, II, V, IV, I, VI    B. I, II, VI, V, III, IV
    C. III, IV, V, I, II, VI    D. V, I, III, VI, IV, II

    1.____

2.  I. If a parent is without assets and is unemployed, he cannot be convicted of the crime of non-support of a child.
    II. The term "sufficient ability" has been held to mean sufficient financial ability.
    III. It does not matter if his unemployment is by choice or unavoidable circumstances.
    IV. If he fails to take any steps at all, he may be liable to prosecution for endangering the welfare of a child.
    V. Under the penal law, a parent is responsible for the support of his minor child only if the parent is "of sufficient ability."
    VI. An indigent parent may meet his obligation by borrowing money or by seeking aid under the provisions of the Social Welfare Law.
    The CORRECT answer is:
    A. VI, I, V, III, II, IV    B. I, III, V, II, IV, VI
    C. V, II, I, III, VI, IV    D. I, VI, IV, V, II, III

    2.____

3.  I. Consider, for example, the case of a rabble rouser who urges a group of twenty people to go out and break the windows of a nearby factory.
    II. Therefore, the law fills the indicated gap with the crime of inciting to riot.
    III. A person is considered guilty of inciting to riot when he urges ten or more persons to engage in tumultuous and violent conduct of a kind likely to create public alarm.
    IV. However, if he has not obtained the cooperation of at least four people, he cannot be charged with unlawful assembly.

    3.____

V. The charge of inciting to riot was added to the law to cover types of conduct which cannot be classified as either the crime of "riot" or the crime of "unlawful assembly."
VI. If he acquires the acquiescence of at least four of them, he is guilty of unlawful assembly even if the project does not materialize.

The CORRECT answer is:
   A. III, V, I, VI, IV, II                 B. V, I, IV, VI, II, III
   C. III, IV, I, V, II, VI                D. V, I, IV, VI, III, II

4.   I. If, however, the rebuttal evidence presents an issue of credibility, it is for the jury to determine whether the presumption has, in fact, been destroyed.
  II. Once sufficient evidence to the contrary is introduced, the presumption disappears from the trial.
  III. The effect of a presumption is to place the burden upon the adversary to come forward with evidence to rebut the presumption.
  IV. When a presumption is overcome and ceases to exist in the case, the fact or facts which gave rise to the presumption still remain.
  V. Whether a presumption has been overcome is ordinarily a question for the court.
  VI. Such information may furnish a basis for a logical inference.

The CORRECT answer is:
   A. IV, VI, II, V, I, III                B. III, II, V, I, IV, VI
   C. V, III, VI, IV, II, I                D. V, IV, I, II, VI, III

---

# KEY (CORRECT ANSWERS)

1. D
2. C
3. A
4. B

# GLOSSARY OF LEGAL TERMS

## TABLE OF CONTENTS

| | Page |
|---|---|
| Action ... Affiant | 1 |
| Affidavit ... At Bar | 2 |
| At Issue ... Burden of Proof | 3 |
| Business ... Commute | 4 |
| Complainant ... Conviction | 5 |
| Cooperative ... Demur (v.) | 6 |
| Demurrage ... Endorsement | 7 |
| Enjoin ... Facsimile | 8 |
| Factor ... Guilty | 9 |
| Habeas Corpus ... Incumbrance | 10 |
| Indemnify ... Laches | 11 |
| Landlord and Tenant ... Malice | 12 |
| Mandamus ... Obiter Dictum | 13 |
| Object (v.) ... Perjury | 14 |
| Perpetuity ... Proclamation | 15 |
| Proffered Evidence ... Referee | 16 |
| Referendum ... Stare Decisis | 17 |
| State ... Term | 18 |
| Testamentary ... Warrant (Warranty) (v.) | 19 |
| Warrant (n.) ... Zoning | 20 |

# GLOSSARY OF LEGAL TERMS

## A

ACTION - "Action" includes a civil action and a criminal action.
A FORTIORI - A term meaning you can reason one thing from the existence of certain facts.
A POSTERIORI - From what goes after; from effect to cause.
A PRIORI - From what goes before; from cause to effect.
AB INITIO - From the beginning.
ABATE - To diminish or put an end to.
ABET - To encourage the commission of a crime.
ABEYANCE - Suspension, temporary suppression.
ABIDE - To accept the consequences of.
ABJURE - To renounce; give up.
ABRIDGE - To reduce; contract; diminish.
ABROGATE - To annul, repeal, or destroy.
ABSCOND - To hide or absent oneself to avoid legal action.
ABSTRACT - A summary.
ABUT - To border on, to touch.
ACCESS - Approach; in real property law it means the right of the owner of property to the use of the highway or road next to his land, without obstruction by intervening property owners.
ACCESSORY - In criminal law, it means the person who contributes or aids in the commission of a crime.
ACCOMMODATED PARTY - One to whom credit is extended on the strength of another person signing a commercial paper.
ACCOMMODATION PAPER - A commercial paper to which the accommodating party has put his name.
ACCOMPLICE - In criminal law, it means a person who together with the principal offender commits a crime.
ACCORD - An agreement to accept something different or less than that to which one is entitled, which extinguishes the entire obligation.
ACCOUNT - A statement of mutual demands in the nature of debt and credit between parties.
ACCRETION - The act of adding to a thing; in real property law, it means gradual accumulation of land by natural causes.
ACCRUE - To grow to; to be added to.
ACKNOWLEDGMENT - The act of going before an official authorized to take acknowledgments, and acknowledging an act as one's own.
ACQUIESCENCE - A silent appearance of consent.
ACQUIT - To legally determine the innocence of one charged with a crime.
AD INFINITUM - Indefinitely.
AD LITEM - For the suit.
AD VALOREM - According to value.
ADJECTIVE LAW - Rules of procedure.
ADJUDICATION - The judgment given in a case.
ADMIRALTY - Court having jurisdiction over maritime cases.
ADULT - Sixteen years old or over (in criminal law).
ADVANCE - In commercial law, it means to pay money or render other value before it is due.
ADVERSE - Opposed; contrary.
ADVOCATE - (v.) To speak in favor of;
          (n.) One who assists, defends, or pleads for another.
AFFIANT - A person who makes and signs an affidavit.

AFFIDAVIT - A written and sworn to declaration of facts, voluntarily made.
AFFINITY- The relationship between persons through marriage with the kindred of each other; distinguished from consanguinity, which is the relationship by blood.
AFFIRM - To ratify; also when an appellate court affirms a judgment, decree, or order, it means that it is valid and right and must stand as rendered in the lower court.
AFOREMENTIONED; AFORESAID - Before or already said.
AGENT - One who represents and acts for another.
AID AND COMFORT - To help; encourage.
ALIAS - A name not one's true name.
ALIBI - A claim of not being present at a certain place at a certain time.
ALLEGE - To assert.
ALLOTMENT - A share or portion.
AMBIGUITY - Uncertainty; capable of being understood in more than one way.
AMENDMENT - Any language made or proposed as a change in some principal writing.
AMICUS CURIAE - A friend of the court; one who has an interest in a case, although not a party in the case, who volunteers advice upon matters of law to the judge. For example, a brief amicus curiae.
AMORTIZATION - To provide for a gradual extinction of (a future obligation) in advance of maturity, especially, by periodical contributions to a sinking fund which will be adequate to discharge a debt or make a replacement when it becomes necessary.
ANCILLARY - Aiding, auxiliary.
ANNOTATION - A note added by way of comment or explanation.
ANSWER - A written statement made by a defendant setting forth the grounds of his defense.
ANTE - Before.
ANTE MORTEM - Before death.
APPEAL - The removal of a case from a lower court to one of superior jurisdiction for the purpose of obtaining a review.
APPEARANCE - Coming into court as a party to a suit.
APPELLANT - The party who takes an appeal from one court or jurisdiction to another (appellate) court for review.
APPELLEE - The party against whom an appeal is taken.
APPROPRIATE - To make a thing one's own.
APPROPRIATION - Prescribing the destination of a thing; the act of the legislature designating a particular fund, to be applied to some object of government expenditure.
APPURTENANT - Belonging to; accessory or incident to.
ARBITER - One who decides a dispute; a referee.
ARBITRARY - Unreasoned; not governed by any fixed rules or standard.
ARGUENDO - By way of argument.
ARRAIGN - To call the prisoner before the court to answer to a charge.
ASSENT - A declaration of willingness to do something in compliance with a request.
ASSERT - Declare.
ASSESS - To fix the rate or amount.
ASSIGN - To transfer; to appoint; to select for a particular purpose.
ASSIGNEE - One who receives an assignment.
ASSIGNOR - One who makes an assignment.
AT BAR - Before the court.

**AT ISSUE** - When parties in an action come to a point where one asserts something and the other denies it.
**ATTACH** - Seize property by court order and sometimes arrest a person.
**ATTEST** - To witness a will, etc.; act of attestation.
**AVERMENT** - A positive statement of facts.

## B

**BAIL** - To obtain the release of a person from legal custody by giving security and promising that he shall appear in court; to deliver (goods, etc.) in trust to a person for a special purpose.
**BAILEE** - One to whom personal property is delivered under a contract of bailment.
**BAILMENT** - Delivery of personal property to another to be held for a certain purpose and to be returned when the purpose is accomplished.
**BAILOR** - The party who delivers goods to another, under a contract of bailment.
**BANC (OR BANK)** - Bench; the place where a court sits permanently or regularly; also the assembly of all the judges of a court.
**BANKRUPT** - An insolvent person, technically, one declared to be bankrupt after a bankruptcy proceeding.
**BAR** - The legal profession.
**BARRATRY** - Exciting groundless judicial proceedings.
**BARTER** - A contract by which parties exchange goods for other goods.
**BATTERY** - Illegal interfering with another's person.
**BEARER** - In commercial law, it means the person in possession of a commercial paper which is payable to the bearer.
**BENCH** - The court itself or the judge.
**BENEFICIARY** - A person benefiting under a will, trust, or agreement.
**BEST EVIDENCE RULE, THE** - Except as otherwise provided by statute, no evidence other than the writing itself is admissible to prove the content of a writing. This section shall be known and may be cited as the best evidence rule.
**BEQUEST** - A gift of personal property under a will.
**BILL** - A formal written statement of complaint to a court of justice; also, a draft of an act of the legislature before it becomes a law; also, accounts for goods sold, services rendered, or work done.
**BONA FIDE** - In or with good faith; honestly.
**BOND** - An instrument by which the maker promises to pay a sum of money to another, usually providing that upon performances of a certain condition the obligation shall be void.
**BOYCOTT** - A plan to prevent the carrying on of a business by wrongful means.
**BREACH** - The breaking or violating of a law, or the failure to carry out a duty.
**BRIEF** - A written document, prepared by a lawyer to serve as the basis of an argument upon a case in court, usually an appellate court.
**BURDEN OF PRODUCING EVIDENCE** - The obligation of a party to introduce evidence sufficient to avoid a ruling against him on the issue.
**BURDEN OF PROOF** - The obligation of a party to establish by evidence a requisite degree of belief concerning a fact in the mind of the trier of fact or the court. The burden of proof may require a party to raise a reasonable doubt concerning the existence of nonexistence of a fact or that he establish the existence or nonexistence of a fact by a preponderance of the evidence, by clear and convincing proof, or by proof beyond a reasonable doubt.

Except as otherwise provided by law, the burden of proof requires proof by a preponderance of the evidence.

BUSINESS, A - Shall include every kind of business, profession, occupation, calling or operation of institutions, whether carried on for profit or not.

BY-LAWS - Regulations, ordinances, or rules enacted by a corporation, association, etc., for its own government.

## C

CANON - A doctrine; also, a law or rule, of a church or association in particular.

CAPIAS - An order to arrest.

CAPTION - In a pleading, deposition or other paper connected with a case in court, it is the heading or introductory clause which shows the names of the parties, name of the court, number of the case on the docket or calendar, etc.

CARRIER - A person or corporation undertaking to transport persons or property.

CASE - A general term for an action, cause, suit, or controversy before a judicial body.

CAUSE - A suit, litigation or action before a court.

CAVEAT EMPTOR - Let the buyer beware. This term expresses the rule that the purchaser of an article must examine, judge, and test it for himself, being bound to discover any obvious defects or imperfections.

CERTIFICATE - A written representation that some legal formality has been complied with.

CERTIORARI - To be informed of; the name of a writ issued by a superior court directing the lower court to send up to the former the record and proceedings of a case.

CHANGE OF VENUE - To remove place of trial from one place to another.

CHARGE - An obligation or duty; a formal complaint; an instruction of the court to the jury upon a case.

CHARTER - (n.) The authority by virtue of which an organized body acts;
 (v.) in mercantile law, it means to hire or lease a vehicle or vessel for transportation.

CHATTEL - An article of personal property.

CHATTEL MORTGAGE - A mortgage on personal property.

CIRCUIT - A division of the country, for the administration of justice; a geographical area served by a court.

CITATION - The act of the court by which a person is summoned or cited; also, a reference to legal authority.

CIVIL (ACTIONS)- It indicates the private rights and remedies of individuals in contrast to the word "criminal" (actions) which relates to prosecution for violation of laws.

CLAIM (n.) - Any demand held or asserted as of right.

CODICIL - An addition to a will.

CODIFY - To arrange the laws of a country into a code.

COGNIZANCE - Notice or knowledge.

COLLATERAL - By the side; accompanying; an article or thing given to secure performance of a promise.

COMITY - Courtesy; the practice by which one court follows the decision of another court on the same question.

COMMIT - To perform, as an act; to perpetrate, as a crime; to send a person to prison.

COMMON LAW - As distinguished from law created by the enactment of the legislature (called statutory law), it relates to those principles and rules of action which derive their authority solely from usages and customs of immemorial antiquity, particularly with reference to the ancient unwritten law of England. The written pronouncements of the common law are found in court decisions.

COMMUTE - Change punishment to one less severe.

COMPLAINANT - One who applies to the court for legal redress.
COMPLAINT - The pleading of a plaintiff in a civil action; or a charge that a person has committed a specified offense.
COMPROMISE - An arrangement for settling a dispute by agreement.
CONCUR - To agree, consent.
CONCURRENT - Running together, at the same time.
CONDEMNATION - Taking private property for public use on payment therefor.
CONDITION - Mode or state of being; a qualification or restriction.
CONDUCT - Active and passive behavior; both verbal and nonverbal.
CONFESSION - Voluntary statement of guilt of crime.
CONFIDENTIAL COMMUNICATION BETWEEN CLIENT AND LAWYER - Information transmitted between a client and his lawyer in the course of that relationship and in confidence by a means which, so far as the client is aware, discloses the information to no third persons other than those who are present to further the interest of the client in the consultation or those to whom disclosure is reasonably necessary for the transmission of the information or the accomplishment of the purpose for which the lawyer is consulted, and includes a legal opinion formed and the advice given by the lawyer in the course of that relationship.
CONFRONTATION - Witness testifying in presence of defendant.
CONSANGUINITY - Blood relationship.
CONSIGN - To give in charge; commit; entrust; to send or transmit goods to a merchant, factor, or agent for sale.
CONSIGNEE - One to whom a consignment is made.
CONSIGNOR - One who sends or makes a consignment.
CONSPIRACY - In criminal law, it means an agreement between two or more persons to commit an unlawful act.
CONSPIRATORS - Persons involved in a conspiracy.
CONSTITUTION - The fundamental law of a nation or state.
CONSTRUCTION OF GENDERS - The masculine gender includes the feminine and neuter.
CONSTRUCTION OF SINGULAR AND PLURAL - The singular number includes the plural; and the plural, the singular.
CONSTRUCTION OF TENSES - The present tense includes the past and future tenses; and the future, the present.
CONSTRUCTIVE - An act or condition assumed from other parts or conditions.
CONSTRUE - To ascertain the meaning of language.
CONSUMMATE - To complete.
CONTIGUOUS - Adjoining; touching; bounded by.
CONTINGENT - Possible, but not assured; dependent upon some condition.
CONTINUANCE - The adjournment or postponement of an action pending in a court.
CONTRA - Against, opposed to; contrary.
CONTRACT - An agreement between two or more persons to do or not to do a particular thing.
CONTROVERT - To dispute, deny.
CONVERSION - Dealing with the personal property of another as if it were one's own, without right.
CONVEYANCE - An instrument transferring title to land.
CONVICTION - Generally, the result of a criminal trial which ends in a judgment or sentence that the defendant is guilty as charged.

COOPERATIVE - A cooperative is a voluntary organization of persons with a common interest, formed and operated along democratic lines for the purpose of supplying services at cost to its members and other patrons, who contribute both capital and business.
CORPUS DELICTI - The body of a crime; the crime itself.
CORROBORATE - To strengthen; to add weight by additional evidence.
COUNTERCLAIM - A claim presented by a defendant in opposition to or deduction from the claim of the plaintiff.
COUNTY - Political subdivision of a state.
COVENANT - Agreement.
CREDIBLE - Worthy of belief.
CREDITOR - A person to whom a debt is owing by another person, called the "debtor."
CRIMINAL ACTION - Includes criminal proceedings.
CRIMINAL INFORMATION - Same as complaint.
CRITERION (sing.)
CRITERIA (plural) - A means or tests for judging; a standard or standards.
CROSS-EXAMINATION - Examination of a witness by a party other than the direct examiner upon a matter that is within the scope of the direct examination of the witness.
CULPABLE - Blamable.
CY-PRES - As near as (possible). The rule of *cy-pres* is a rule for the construction of instruments in equity by which the intention of the party is carried out *as near as may be*, when it would be impossible or illegal to give it literal effect.

## D

DAMAGES - A monetary compensation, which may be recovered in the courts by any person who has suffered loss, or injury, whether to his person, property or rights through the unlawful act or omission or negligence of another.
DECLARANT - A person who makes a statement.
DE FACTO - In fact; actually but without legal authority.
DE JURE - Of right; legitimate; lawful.
DE MINIMIS - Very small or trifling.
DE NOVO - Anew; afresh; a second time.
DEBT - A specified sum of money owing to one person from another, including not only the obligation of the debtor to pay, but the right of the creditor to receive and enforce payment.
DECEDENT - A dead person.
DECISION - A judgment or decree pronounced by a court in determination of a case.
DECREE - An order of the court, determining the rights of all parties to a suit.
DEED - A writing containing a contract sealed and delivered; particularly to convey real property.
DEFALCATION - Misappropriation of funds.
DEFAMATION - Injuring one's reputation by false statements.
DEFAULT - The failure to fulfill a duty, observe a promise, discharge an obligation, or perform an agreement.
DEFENDANT - The person defending or denying; the party against whom relief or recovery is sought in an action or suit.
DEFRAUD - To practice fraud; to cheat or trick.
DELEGATE (v.)- To entrust to the care or management of another.
DELICTUS - A crime.
DEMUR (v.) - To dispute the sufficiency in law of the pleading of the other side.

DEMURRAGE - In maritime law, it means, the sum fixed or allowed as remuneration to the owners of a ship for the detention of their vessel beyond the number of days allowed for loading and unloading or for sailing; also used in railroad terminology.
DENIAL - A form of pleading; refusing to admit the truth of a statement, charge, etc.
DEPONENT - One who gives testimony under oath reduced to writing.
DEPOSITION - Testimony given under oath outside of court for use in court or for the purpose of obtaining information in preparation for trial of a case.
DETERIORATION - A degeneration such as from decay, corrosion or disintegration.
DETRIMENT - Any loss or harm to person or property.
DEVIATION - A turning aside.
DEVISE - A gift of real property by the last will and testament of the donor.
DICTUM (sing.)
DICTA (plural) - Any statements made by the court in an opinion concerning some rule of law not necessarily involved nor essential to the determination of the case.
DIRECT EVIDENCE - Evidence that directly proves a fact, without an inference or presumption, and which in itself if true, conclusively establishes that fact.
DIRECT EXAMINATION - The first examination of a witness upon a matter that is not within the scope of a previous examination of the witness.
DISAFFIRM - To repudiate.
DISMISS - In an action or suit, it means to dispose of the case without any further consideration or hearing.
DISSENT - To denote disagreement of one or more judges of a court with the decision passed by the majority upon a case before them.
DOCKET (n.) - A formal record, entered in brief, of the proceedings in a court.
DOCTRINE - A rule, principle, theory of law.
DOMICILE - That place where a man has his true, fixed and permanent home to which whenever he is absent he has the intention of returning.
DRAFT (n.) - A commercial paper ordering payment of money drawn by one person on another.
DRAWEE - The person who is requested to pay the money.
DRAWER - The person who draws the commercial paper and addresses it to the drawee.
DUPLICATE - A counterpart produced by the same impression as the original enlargements and miniatures, or by mechanical or electronic re-recording, or by chemical reproduction, or by other equivalent technique which accurately reproduces the original.
DURESS - Use of force to compel performance or non-performance of an act.

## E

EASEMENT - A liberty, privilege, or advantage without profit, in the lands of another.
EGRESS - Act or right of going out or leaving; emergence.
EIUSDEM GENERIS - Of the same kind, class or nature. A rule used in the construction of language in a legal document.
EMBEZZLEMENT - To steal; to appropriate fraudulently to one's own use property entrusted to one's care.
EMBRACERY - Unlawful attempt to influence jurors, etc., but not by offering value.
EMINENT DOMAIN - The right of a state to take private property for public use.
ENACT - To make into a law.
ENDORSEMENT - Act of writing one's name on the back of a note, bill or similar written instrument.

ENJOIN - To require a person, by writ of injunction from a court of equity, to perform or to abstain or desist from some act.
ENTIRETY - The whole; that which the law considers as one whole, and not capable of being divided into parts.
ENTRAPMENT - Inducing one to commit a crime so as to arrest him.
ENUMERATED - Mentioned specifically; designated.
ENURE - To operate or take effect.
EQUITY - In its broadest sense, this term denotes the spirit and the habit of fairness, justness, and right dealing which regulate the conduct of men.
ERROR - A mistake of law, or the false or irregular application of law as will nullify the judicial proceedings.
ESCROW - A deed, bond or other written engagement, delivered to a third person, to be delivered by him only upon the performance or fulfillment of some condition.
ESTATE - The interest which any one has in lands, or in any other subject of property.
ESTOP - To stop, bar, or impede.
ESTOPPEL - A rule of law which prevents a man from alleging or denying a fact, because of his own previous act.
ET AL. (alii) - And others.
ET SEQ. (sequential) - And the following.
ET UX. (uxor) - And wife.
EVIDENCE - Testimony, writings, material objects, or other things presented to the senses that are offered to prove the existence or non-existence of a fact.
   Means from which inferences may be drawn as a basis of proof in duly constituted judicial or fact finding tribunals, and includes testimony in the form of opinion and hearsay.
EX CONTRACTU
EX DELICTO - In law, rights and causes of action are divided into two classes, those arising *ex contractu* (from a contract) and those arising *ex delicto* (from a delict or tort).
EX OFFICIO - From office; by virtue of the office.
EX PARTE - On one side only; by or for one.
EX POST FACTO - After the fact.
EX POST FACTO LAW - A law passed after an act was done which retroactively makes such act a crime.
EX REL. (relations) - Upon relation or information.
EXCEPTION - An objection upon a matter of law to a decision made, either before or after judgment by a court.
EXECUTOR (male)
EXECUTRIX (female) - A person who has been appointed by will to execute the will.
EXECUTORY - That which is yet to be executed or performed.
EXEMPT - To release from some liability to which others are subject.
EXONERATION - The removal of a burden, charge or duty.
EXTRADITION - Surrender of a fugitive from one nation to another.

# F

F.A.S.- "Free alongside ship"; delivery at dock for ship named.
F.O.B.- "Free on board"; seller will deliver to car, truck, vessel, or other conveyance by which goods are to be transported, without expense or risk of loss to the buyer or consignee.
FABRICATE - To construct; to invent a false story.
FACSIMILE - An exact or accurate copy of an original instrument.

FACTOR - A commercial agent.
FEASANCE - The doing of an act.
FELONIOUS - Criminal, malicious.
FELONY - Generally, a criminal offense that may be punished by death or imprisonment for more than one year as differentiated from a misdemeanor.
FEME SOLE - A single woman.
FIDUCIARY - A person who is invested with rights and powers to be exercised for the benefit of another person.
FIERI FACIAS - A writ of execution commanding the sheriff to levy and collect the amount of a judgment from the goods and chattels of the judgment debtor.
FINDING OF FACT - Determination from proof or judicial notice of the existence of a fact. A ruling implies a supporting finding of fact; no separate or formal finding is required unless required by a statute of this state.
FISCAL - Relating to accounts or the management of revenue.
FORECLOSURE (sale) - A sale of mortgaged property to obtain satisfaction of the mortgage out of the sale proceeds.
FORFEITURE - A penalty, a fine.
FORGERY - Fabricating or producing falsely, counterfeited.
FORTUITOUS - Accidental.
FORUM - A court of justice; a place of jurisdiction.
FRAUD - Deception; trickery.
FREEHOLDER - One who owns real property.
FUNGIBLE - Of such kind or nature that one specimen or part may be used in the place of another.

## G

GARNISHEE - Person garnished.
GARNISHMENT - A legal process to reach the money or effects of a defendant, in the possession or control of a third person.
GRAND JURY - Not less than 16, not more than 23 citizens of a county sworn to inquire into crimes committed or triable in the county.
GRANT - To agree to; convey, especially real property.
GRANTEE - The person to whom a grant is made.
GRANTOR - The person by whom a grant is made.
GRATUITOUS - Given without a return, compensation or consideration.
GRAVAMEN - The grievance complained of or the substantial cause of a criminal action.
GUARANTY (n.) - A promise to answer for the payment of some debt, or the performance of some duty, in case of the failure of another person, who, in the first instance, is liable for such payment or performance.
GUARDIAN - The person, committee, or other representative authorized by law to protect the person or estate or both of an incompetent (or of a *sui juris* person having a guardian) and to act for him in matters affecting his person or property or both. An incompetent is a person under disability imposed by law.
GUILTY - Establishment of the fact that one has committed a breach of conduct; especially, a violation of law.

## H

HABEAS CORPUS - You have the body; the name given to a variety of writs, having for their object to bring a party before a court or judge for decision as to whether such person is being lawfully held prisoner.
HABENDUM - In conveyancing; it is the clause in a deed conveying land which defines the extent of ownership to be held by the grantee.
HEARING - A proceeding whereby the arguments of the interested parties are heared.
HEARSAY - A type of testimony given by a witness who relates, not what he knows personally, but what others have told hi, or what he has heard said by others.
HEARSAY RULE, THE - (a) "Hearsay evidence" is evidence of a statement that was made other than by a witness while testifying at the hearing and that is offered to prove the truth of the matter stated; (b) Except as provided by law, hearsay evidence is inadmissible; (c) This section shall be known and may be cited as the hearsay rule.
HEIR - Generally, one who inherits property, real or personal.
HOLDER OF THE PRIVILEGE - (a) The client when he has no guardian or conservator; (b) A guardian or conservator of the client when the client has a guardian or conservator; (c) The personal representative of the client if the client is dead; (d) A successor, assign, trustee in dissolution, or any similar representative of a firm, association, organization, partnership, business trust, corporation, or public entity that is no longer in existence.
HUNG JURY - One so divided that they can't agree on a verdict.
HUSBAND-WIFE PRIVILEGE - An accused in a criminal proceeding has a privilege to prevent his spouse from testifying against him.
HYPOTHECATE - To pledge a thing without delivering it to the pledgee.
HYPOTHESIS - A supposition, assumption, or toehry.

## I

I.E. (id est) - That is.
IB., OR IBID.(ibidem) - In the same place; used to refer to a legal reference previously cited to avoid repeating the entire citation.
ILLICIT - Prohibited; unlawful.
ILLUSORY - Deceiving by false appearance.
IMMUNITY - Exemption.
IMPEACH - To accuse, to dispute.
IMPEDIMENTS - Disabilities, or hindrances.
IMPLEAD - To sue or prosecute by due course of law.
IMPUTED - Attributed or charged to.
IN LOCO PARENTIS - In place of parent, a guardian.
IN TOTO - In the whole; completely.
INCHOATE - Imperfect; unfinished.
INCOMMUNICADO - Denial of the right of a prisoner to communicate with friends or relatives.
INCOMPETENT - One who is incapable of caring for his own affairs because he is mentally deficient or undeveloped.
INCRIMINATION - A matter will incriminate a person if it constitutes, or forms an essential part of, or, taken in connection with other matters disclosed, is a basis for a reasonable inference of such a violation of the laws of this State as to subject him to liability to punishment therefor, unless he has become for any reason permanently immune from punishment for such violation.
INCUMBRANCE - Generally a claim, lien, charge or liability attached to and binding real property.

INDEMNIFY - To secure against loss or damage; also, to make reimbursement to one for a loss already incurred by him.
INDEMNITY - An agreement to reimburse another person in case of an anticipated loss falling upon him.
INDICIA - Signs; indications.
INDICTMENT - An accusation in writing found and presented by a grand jury charging that a person has committed a crime.
INDORSE - To write a name on the back of a legal paper or document, generally, a negotiable instrument
INDUCEMENT - Cause or reason why a thing is done or that which incites the person to do the act or commit a crime; the motive for the criminal act.
INFANT - In civil cases one under 21 years of age.
INFORMATION - A formal accusation of crime made by a prosecuting attorney.
INFRA - Below, under; this word occurring by itself in a publication refers the reader to a future part of the publication.
INGRESS - The act of going into.
INJUNCTION - A writ or order by the court requiring a person, generally, to do or to refrain from doing an act.
INSOLVENT - The condition of a person who is unable to pay his debts.
INSTRUCTION - A direction given by the judge to the jury concerning the law of the case.
INTERIM - In the meantime; time intervening.
INTERLOCUTORY - Temporary, not final; something intervening between the commencement and the end of a suit which decides some point or matter, but is not a final decision of the whole controversy.
INTERROGATORIES - A series of formal written questions used in the examination of a party or a witness usually prior to a trial.
INTESTATE - A person who dies without a will.
INURE - To result, to take effect.
IPSO FACTO - By the fact iself; by the mere fact.
ISSUE (n.) The disputed point or question in a case,

## J

JEOPARDY - Danger, hazard, peril.
JOINDER - Joining; uniting with another person in some legal steps or proceeding.
JOINT - United; combined.
JUDGE - Member or members or representative or representatives of a court conducting a trial or hearing at which evidence is introduced.
JUDGMENT - The official decision of a court of justice.
JUDICIAL OR JUDICIARY - Relating to or connected with the administration of justice.
JURAT - The clause written at the foot of an affidavit, stating when, where and before whom such affidavit was sworn.
JURISDICTION - The authority to hear and determine controversies between parties.
JURISPRUDENCE - The philosophy of law.
JURY - A body of persons legally selected to inquire into any matter of fact, and to render their verdict according to the evidence.

## L

LACHES - The failure to diligently assert a right, which results in a refusal to allow relief.

LANDLORD AND TENANT - A phrase used to denote the legal relation existing between the owner and occupant of real estate.

LARCENY - Stealing personal property belonging to another.

LATENT - Hidden; that which does not appear on the face of a thing.

LAW - Includes constitutional, statutory, and decisional law.

LAWYER-CLIENT PRIVILEGE - (1) A "client" is a person, public officer, or corporation, association, or other organization or entity, either public or private, who is rendered professional legal services by a lawyer, or who consults a lawyer with a view to obtaining professional legal services from him; (2) A "lawyer" is a person authorized, or reasonably believed by the client to be authorized, to practice law in any state or nation; (3) A "representative of the lawyer" is one employed to assist the lawyer in the rendition of professional legal services; (4) A communication is "confidential" if not intended to be disclosed to third persons other than those to whom disclosure is in furtherance of the rendition of professional legal services to the client or those reasonably necessary for the transmission of the communication.

*General rule of privilege* - A client has a privilege to refuse to disclose and to prevent any other person from disclosing confidential communications made for the purpose of facilitating the rendition of professional legal services to the client, (1) between himself or his representative and his lawyer or his lawyer's representative, or (2) between his lawyer and the lawyer's representative, or (3) by him or his lawyer to a lawyer representing another in a matter of common interest, or (4) between representatives of the client or between the client and a representative of the client, or (5) between lawyers representing the client.

LEADING QUESTION - Question that suggests to the witness the answer that the examining party desires.

LEASE - A contract by which one conveys real estate for a limited time usually for a specified rent; personal property also may be leased.

LEGISLATION - The act of enacting laws.

LEGITIMATE - Lawful.

LESSEE - One to whom a lease is given.

LESSOR - One who grants a lease

LEVY - A collecting or exacting by authority.

LIABLE - Responsible; bound or obligated in law or equity.

LIBEL (v.) - To defame or injure a person's reputation by a published writing.

(n.) - The initial pleading on the part of the plaintiff in an admiralty proceeding.

LIEN - A hold or claim which one person has upon the property of another as a security for some debt or charge.

LIQUIDATED - Fixed; settled.

LIS PENDENS - A pending civil or criminal action.

LITERAL - According to the language.

LITIGANT - A party to a lawsuit.

LITATION - A judicial controversy.

LOCUS - A place.

LOCUS DELICTI - Place of the crime.

LOCUS POENITENTIAE - The abandoning or giving up of one's intention to commit some crime before it is fully completed or abandoning a conspiracy before its purpose is accomplished.

## M

MALFEASANCE - To do a wrongful act.

MALICE - The doing of a wrongful act Intentionally without just cause or excuse.

MANDAMUS - The name of a writ issued by a court to enforce the performance of some public duty.
MANDATORY (adj.) Containing a command.
MARITIME - Pertaining to the sea or to commerce thereon.
MARSHALING - Arranging or disposing of in order.
MAXIM - An established principle or proposition.
MINISTERIAL - That which involves obedience to instruction, but demands no special discretion, judgment or skill.
MISAPPROPRIATE - Dealing fraudulently with property entrusted to one.
MISDEMEANOR - A crime less than a felony and punishable by a fine or imprisonment for less than one year.
MISFEASANCE - Improper performance of a lawful act.
MISREPRESENTATION - An untrue representation of facts.
MITIGATE - To make or become less severe, harsh.
MITTIMUS - A warrant of commitment to prison.
MOOT (adj.) Unsettled, undecided, not necessary to be decided.
MORTGAGE - A conveyance of property upon condition, as security for the payment of a debt or the performance of a duty, and to become void upon payment or performance according to the stipulated terms.
MORTGAGEE - A person to whom property is mortgaged.
MORTGAGOR - One who gives a mortgage.
MOTION - In legal proceedings, a "motion" is an application, either written or oral, addressed to the court by a party to an action or a suit requesting the ruling of the court on a matter of law.
MUTUALITY - Reciprocation.

## N

NEGLIGENCE - The failure to exercise that degree of care which an ordinarily prudent person would exercise under like circumstances.
NEGOTIABLE (instrument) - Any instrument obligating the payment of money which is transferable from one person to another by endorsement and delivery or by delivery only.
NEGOTIATE - To transact business; to transfer a negotiable instrument; to seek agreement for the amicable disposition of a controversy or case.
NOLLE PROSEQUI - A formal entry upon the record, by the plaintiff in a civil suit or the prosecuting officer in a criminal action, by which he declares that he "will no further prosecute" the case.
NOLO CONTENDERE - The name of a plea in a criminal action, having the same effect as a plea of guilty; but not constituting a direct admission of guilt.
NOMINAL - Not real or substantial.
NOMINAL DAMAGES - Award of a trifling sum where no substantial injury is proved to have been sustained.
NONFEASANCE - Neglect of duty.
NOVATION - The substitution of a new debt or obligation for an existing one.
NUNC PRO TUNC - A phrase applied to acts allowed to be done after the time when they should be done, with a retroactive effect.("Now for then.")

## O

OATH - Oath includes affirmation or declaration under penalty of perjury.
OBITER DICTUM - Opinion expressed by a court on a matter not essentially involved in a case and hence not a decision; also called dicta, if plural.

OBJECT (v.) - To oppose as improper or illegal and referring the question of its propriety or legality to the court.
OBLIGATION - A legal duty, by which a person is bound to do or not to do a certain thing.
OBLIGEE - The person to whom an obligation is owed.
OBLIGOR - The person who is to perform the obligation.
OFFER (v.) - To present for acceptance or rejection.
    (n.) - A proposal to do a thing, usually a proposal to make a contract.
OFFICIAL INFORMATION - Information within the custody or control of a department or agency of the government the disclosure of which is shown to be contrary to the public interest.
OFFSET - A deduction.
ONUS PROBANDI - Burden of proof.
OPINION - The statement by a judge of the decision reached in a case, giving the law as applied to the case and giving reasons for the judgment; also a belief or view.
OPTION - The exercise of the power of choice; also a privilege existing in one person, for which he has paid money, which gives him the right to buy or sell real or personal property at a given price within a specified time.
ORDER - A rule or regulation; every direction of a court or judge made or entered in writing but not including a judgment.
ORDINANCE - Generally, a rule established by authority; also commonly used to designate the legislative acts of a municipal corporation.
ORIGINAL - Writing or recording itself or any counterpart intended to have the same effect by a person executing or issuing it. An "original" of a photograph includes the negative or any print therefrom. If data are stored in a computer or similar device, any printout or other output readable by sight, shown to reflect the data accurately, is an "original."
OVERT - Open, manifest.

**P**

PANEL - A group of jurors selected to serve during a term of the court.
PARENS PATRIAE - Sovereign power of a state to protect or be a guardian over children and incompetents.
PAROL - Oral or verbal.
PAROLE - To release one in prison before the expiration of his sentence, conditionally.
PARITY - Equality in purchasing power between the farmer and other segments of the economy.
PARTITION - A legal division of real or personal property between one or more owners.
PARTNERSHIP - An association of two or more persons to carry on as co-owners a business for profit.
PATENT (adj.) - Evident.
    (n.) - A grant of some privilege, property, or authority, made by the government or sovereign of a country to one or more individuals.
PECULATION - Stealing.
PECUNIARY - Monetary.
PENULTIMATE - Next to the last.
PER CURIAM - A phrase used in the report of a decision to distinguish an opinion of the whole court from an opinion written by any one judge.
PER SE - In itself; taken alone.
PERCEIVE - To acquire knowledge through one's senses.
PEREMPTORY - Imperative; absolute.
PERJURY - To lie or state falsely under oath.

PERPETUITY - Perpetual existence; also the quality or condition of an estate limited so that it will not take effect or vest within the period fixed by law.
PERSON - Includes a natural person, firm, association, organization, partnership, business trust, corporation, or public entity.
PERSONAL PROPERTY - Includes money, goods, chattels, things in action, and evidences of debt.
PERSONALTY - Short term for personal property.
PETITION - An application in writing for an order of the court, stating the circumstances upon which it is founded and requesting any order or other relief from a court.
PLAINTIFF - A person who brings a court action.
PLEA - A pleading in a suit or action.
PLEADINGS - Formal allegations made by the parties of their respective claims and defenses, for the judgment of the court.
PLEDGE - A deposit of personal property as a security for the performance of an act.
PLEDGEE - The party to whom goods are delivered in pledge.
PLEDGOR - The party delivering goods in pledge.
PLENARY - Full; complete.
POLICE POWER - Inherent power of the state or its political subdivisions to enact laws within constitutional limits to promote the general welfare of society or the community.
POLLING THE JURY - Call the names of persons on a jury and requiring each juror to declare what his verdict is before it is legally recorded.
POST MORTEM - After death.
POWER OF ATTORNEY - A writing authorizing one to act for another.
PRECEPT - An order, warrant, or writ issued to an officer or body of officers, commanding him or them to do some act within the scope of his or their powers.
PRELIMINARY FACT - Fact upon the existence or nonexistence of which depends the admissibility or inadmissibility of evidence. The phrase "the admissibility or inadmissibility of evidence" includes the qualification or disqualification of a person to be a witness and the existence or nonexistence of a privilege.
PREPONDERANCE - Outweighing.
PRESENTMENT - A report by a grand jury on something they have investigated on their own knowledge.
PRESUMPTION - An assumption of fact resulting from a rule of law which requires such fact to be assumed from another fact or group of facts found or otherwise established in the action.
PRIMA FACUE - At first sight.
PRIMA FACIE CASE - A case where the evidence is very patent against the defendant.
PRINCIPAL - The source of authority or rights; a person primarily liable as differentiated from "principle" as a primary or basic doctrine.
PRO AND CON - For and against.
PRO RATA - Proportionally.
PROBATE - Relating to proof, especially to the proof of wills.
PROBATIVE - Tending to prove.
PROCEDURE - In law, this term generally denotes rules which are established by the Federal, State, or local Governments regarding the types of pleading and courtroom practice which must be followed by the parties involved in a criminal or civil case.
PROCLAMATION - A public notice by an official of some order, intended action, or state of facts.

PROFFERED EVIDENCE - The admissibility or inadmissibility of which is dependent upon the existence or nonexistence of a preliminary fact.

PROMISSORY (NOTE) - A promise in writing to pay a specified sum at an expressed time, or on demand, or at sight, to a named person, or to his order, or bearer.

PROOF - The establishment by evidence of a requisite degree of belief concerning a fact in the mind of the trier of fact or the court.

PROPERTY - Includes both real and personal property.

PROPRIETARY (adj.) - Relating or pertaining to ownership; usually a single owner.

PROSECUTE - To carry on an action or other judicial proceeding; to proceed against a person criminally.

PROVISO - A limitation or condition in a legal instrument.

PROXIMATE - Immediate; nearest

PUBLIC EMPLOYEE - An officer, agent, or employee of a public entity.

PUBLIC ENTITY - Includes a national, state, county, city and county, city, district, public authority, public agency, or any other political subdivision or public corporation, whether foreign or domestic.

PUBLIC OFFICIAL - Includes an official of a political dubdivision of such state or territory and of a municipality.

PUNITIVE - Relating to punishment.

## Q

QUASH - To make void.

QUASI - As if; as it were.

QUID PRO QUO - Something for something; the giving of one valuable thing for another.

QUITCLAIM (v.) - To release or relinquish claim or title to, especially in deeds to realty.

QUO WARRANTO - A legal procedure to test an official's right to a public office or the right to hold a franchise, or to hold an office in a domestic corporation.

## R

RATIFY - To approve and sanction.

REAL PROPERTY - Includes lands, tenements, and hereditaments.

REALTY - A brief term for real property.

REBUT - To contradict; to refute, especially by evidence and arguments.

RECEIVER - A person who is appointed by the court to receive, and hold in trust property in litigation.

RECIDIVIST - Habitual criminal.

RECIPROCAL - Mutual.

RECOUPMENT - To keep back or get something which is due; also, it is the right of a defendant to have a deduction from the amount of the plaintiff's damages because the plaintiff has not fulfilled his part of the same contract.

RECROSS EXAMINATION - Examination of a witness by a cross-examiner subsequent to a redirect examination of the witness.

REDEEM - To release an estate or article from mortgage or pledge by paying the debt for which it stood as security.

REDIRECT EXAMINATION - Examination of a witness by the direct examiner subsequent to the cross-examination of the witness.

REFEREE - A person to whom a cause pending in a court is referred by the court, to take testimony, hear the parties, and report thereon to the court.

REFERENDUM - A method of submitting an important legislative or administrative matter to a direct vote of the people.
RELEVANT EVIDENCE - Evidence including evidence relevant to the credulity of a witness or hearsay declarant, having any tendency in reason to prove or disprove any disputed fact that is of consequence to the determination of the action.
REMAND - To send a case back to the lower court from which it came, for further proceedings.
REPLEVIN - An action to recover goods or chattels wrongfully taken or detained.
REPLY (REPLICATION) - Generally, a reply is what the plaintiff or other person who has instituted proceedings says in answer to the defendant's case.
RE JUDICATA - A thing judicially acted upon or decided.
RES ADJUDICATA - Doctrine that an issue or dispute litigated and determined in a case between the opposing parties is deemed permanently decided between these parties.
RESCIND (RECISSION) - To avoid or cancel a contract.
RESPONDENT - A defendant in a proceeding in chancery or admiralty; also, the person who contends against the appeal in a case.
RESTITUTION - In equity, it is the restoration of both parties to their original condition (when practicable), upon the rescission of a contract for fraud or similar cause.
RETROACTIVE (RETROSPECTIVE) - Looking back; effective as of a prior time.
REVERSED - A term used by appellate courts to indicate that the decision of the lower court in the case before it has been set aside.
REVOKE - To recall or cancel.
RIPARIAN (RIGHTS) - The rights of a person owning land containing or bordering on a water course or other body of water, such as lakes and rivers.

## S

SALE - A contract whereby the ownership of property is transferred from one person to another for a sum of money or for any consideration.
SANCTION - A penalty or punishment provided as a means of enforcing obedience to a law; also, an authorization.
SATISFACTION - The discharge of an obligation by paying a party what is due to him; or what is awarded to him by the judgment of a court or otherwise.
SCIENTER - Knowingly; also, it is used in pleading to denote the defendant's guilty knowledge.
SCINTILLA - A spark; also the least particle.
SECRET OF STATE - Governmental secret relating to the national defense or the international relations of the United States.
SECURITY - Indemnification; the term is applied to an obligation, such as a mortgage or deed of trust, given by a debtor to insure the payment or performance of his debt, by furnishing the creditor with a resource to be used in case of the debtor's failure to fulfill the principal obligation.
SENTENCE - The judgment formally pronounced by the court or judge upon the defendant after his conviction in a criminal prosecution.
SET-OFF - A claim or demand which one party in an action credits against the claim of the opposing party.
SHALL and MAY - "Shall" is mandatory and "may" is permissive.
SITUS - Location.
SOVEREIGN - A person, body or state in which independent and supreme authority is vested.
STARE DECISIS - To follow decided cases.

STATE - "State" means this State, unless applied to the different parts of the United States. In the latter case, it includes any state, district, commonwealth, territory or insular possession of the United States, including the District of Columbia.

STATEMENT - (a) Oral or written verbal expression or (b) nonverbal conduct of a person intended by him as a substitute for oral or written verbal expression.

STATUTE - An act of the legislature. Includes a treaty.

STATUTE OF LIMITATION - A statute limiting the time to bring an action after the right of action has arisen.

STAY - To hold in abeyance an order of a court.

STIPULATION - Any agreement made by opposing attorneys regulating any matter incidental to the proceedings or trial.

SUBORDINATION (AGREEMENT) - An agreement making one's rights inferior to or of a lower rank than another's.

SUBORNATION - The crime of procuring a person to lie or to make false statements to a court.

SUBPOENA - A writ or order directed to a person, and requiring his attendance at a particular time and place to testify as a witness.

SUBPOENA DUCES TECUM - A subpoena used, not only for the purpose of compelling witnesses to attend in court, but also requiring them to bring with them books or documents which may be in their possession, and which may tend to elucidate the subject matter of the trial.

SUBROGATION - The substituting of one for another as a creditor, the new creditor succeeding to the former's rights.

SUBSIDY - A government grant to assist a private enterprise deemed advantageous to the public.

SUI GENERIS - Of the same kind.

SUIT - Any civil proceeding by a person or persons against another or others in a court of justice by which the plaintiff pursues the remedies afforded him by law.

SUMMONS - A notice to a defendant that an action against him has been commenced and requiring him to appear in court and answer the complaint.

SUPRA - Above; this word occurring by itself in a book refers the reader to a previous part of the book.

SURETY - A person who binds himself for the payment of a sum of money, or for the performance of something else, for another.

SURPLUSAGE - Extraneous or unnecessary matter.

SURVIVORSHIP - A term used when a person becomes entitled to property by reason of his having survived another person who had an interest in the property.

SUSPEND SENTENCE - Hold back a sentence pending good behavior of prisoner.

SYLLABUS - A note prefixed to a report, especially a case, giving a brief statement of the court's ruling on different issues of the case.

## T

TALESMAN - Person summoned to fill a panel of jurors.

TENANT - One who holds or possesses lands by any kind of right or title; also, one who has the temporary use and occupation of real property owned by another person (landlord), the duration and terms of his tenancy being usually fixed by an instrument called "a lease."

TENDER - An offer of money; an expression of willingness to perform a contract according to its terms.

TERM - When used with reference to a court, it signifies the period of time during which the court holds a session, usually of several weeks or months duration.

TESTAMENTARY - Pertaining to a will or the administration of a will.
TESTATOR (male)
TESTATRIX (female) - One who makes or has made a testament or will.
TESTIFY (TESTIMONY) - To give evidence under oath as a witness.
TO WIT - That is to say; namely.
TORT - Wrong; injury to the person.
TRANSITORY - Passing from place to place.
TRESPASS - Entry into another's ground, illegally.
TRIAL - The examination of a cause, civil or criminal, before a judge who has jurisdiction over it, according to the laws of the land.
TRIER OF FACT - Includes (a) the jury and (b) the court when the court is trying an issue of fact other than one relating to the admissibility of evidence.
TRUST - A right of property, real or personal, held by one party for the benefit of another.
TRUSTEE - One who lawfully holds property in custody for the benefit of another.

## U

UNAVAILABLE AS A WITNESS - The declarant is (1) Exempted or precluded on the ground of privilege from testifying concerning the matter to which his statement is relevant; (2) Disqualified from testifying to the matter; (3) Dead or unable to attend or to testify at the hearing because of then existing physical or mental illness or infirmity; (4) Absent from the hearing and the court is unable to compel his attendance by its process; or (5) Absent from the hearing and the proponent of his statement has exercised reasonable diligence but has been unable to procure his attendance by the court's process.
ULTRA VIRES - Acts beyond the scope and power of a corporation, association, etc.
UNILATERAL - One-sided; obligation upon, or act of one party.
USURY - Unlawful interest on a loan.

## V

VACATE - To set aside; to move out.
VARIANCE - A discrepancy or disagreement between two instruments or two aspects of the same case, which by law should be consistent.
VENDEE - A purchaser or buyer.
VENDOR - The person who transfers property by sale, particularly real estate; the term "seller" is used more commonly for one who sells personal property.
VENIREMEN - Persons ordered to appear to serve on a jury or composing a panel of jurors.
VENUE - The place at which an action is tried, generally based on locality or judicial district in which an injury occurred or a material fact happened.
VERDICT - The formal decision or finding of a jury.
VERIFY - To confirm or substantiate by oath.
VEST - To accrue to.
VOID - Having no legal force or binding effect.
VOIR DIRE - Preliminary examination of a witness or a juror to test competence, interest, prejudice, etc.

## W

WAIVE - To give up a right.
WAIVER - The intentional or voluntary relinquishment of a known right.
WARRANT (WARRANTY) (v.) - To promise that a certain fact or state of facts, in relation to the subject matter, is, or shall be, as it is represented to be.

WARRANT (n.) - A writ issued by a judge, or other competent authority, addressed to a sheriff, or other officer, requiring him to arrest the person therein named, and bring him before the judge or court to answer or be examined regarding the offense with which he is charged.

WRIT - An order or process issued in the name of the sovereign or in the name of a court or judicial officer, commanding the performance or nonperformance of some act.

WRITING - Handwriting, typewriting, printing, photostating, photographing and every other means of recording upon any tangible thing any form of communication or representation, including letters, words, pictures, sounds, or symbols, or combinations thereof.

WRITINGS AND RECORDINGS - Consists of letters, words, or numbers, or their equivalent, set down by handwriting, typewriting, printing, photostating, photographing, magnetic impulse, mechanical or electronic recording, or other form of data compilation.

## Y

YEA AND NAY - Yes and no.

YELLOW DOG CONTRACT - A contract by which employer requires employee to sign an instrument promising as condition that he will not join a union during its continuance, and will be discharged if he does join.

## Z

ZONING - The division of a city by legislative regulation into districts and the prescription and application in each district of regulations having to do with structural and architectural designs of buildings and of regulations prescribing use to which buildings within designated districts may be put.

www.ingramcontent.com/pod-product-compliance
Lightning Source LLC
Chambersburg PA
CBHW081829300426
44116CB00014B/2528